CAREERS FOR WOMEN IN POLITICS

CAREERS FOR WOMEN IN POLITICS

By
Richard S. Lee
and
Mary Price Lee

St. Mary Regional High School
Library
310 Augusta Street
South Amboy, New Jersey 08879

THE ROSEN PUBLISHING GROUP, Inc.
New York

Published in 1989 by The Rosen Publishing Group, Inc.
29 East 21st Street, New York, NY 10010

Copyright 1989 by Richard S. and Mary Price Lee

All rights reserved. No part of this book may be reproduced in any form without permission in writing from the publisher, except by a reviewer.

First Edition

Library of Congress Cataloging-In-Publication Data

Lee, Richard S. (Richard Sandoval), 1922–
  Careers for women in politics / by Richard S. Lee and Mary Price Lee.
    p. cm.
  Bibliography: p.
  Includes index.
  ISBN 0-8239-0966-2
  1. Women in politics—United States—Juvenile literature. 2. Politics, Practical—Vocational guidance—United States—Juvenile literature.
3. Career development—United States—Juvenile literature. I. Lee, Mary Price. II. Title.
HQ1236.5.U6L44 1989
320'.024042—dc20   89-6320
                                              CIP
                                              AC

Manufactured in the United States of America

To
Julie Sten,
whose radiant enthusiasm
is a pleasure to us all.

Contents

	Preface	ix
	Acknowledgments	xi
I.	*Your Future in Politics*	1
II.	*Politics Is Tough—but So Are Women!*	3
III.	*The Woman Politician: Sugar and Spice*	7
IV.	*Junior High and High School*	11
V.	*College*	23
VI.	*Financial Resources for Political Study*	33
VII.	*Fighting the Myths and Considering a Run*	37
VIII.	*Running for Office*	45
IX.	*Local Government*	51
X.	*State Politics*	61
XI.	*The Rare Nine: Women Governors*	73
XII.	*National Political Office*	79
XIII.	*A Women's Hall of Fame*	89
XIV.	*Nonelective Politics*	99
XV.	*Where Do You Go From Here?*	105
	Appendix 1: Women in Public Office	109
	Appendix 2: Women's Political Organizations	119
	Bibliography	121
	Index	123

Preface

This is a book about career prospects and realities for women in political office. Winning elective office is one of many ways women can serve the public in a political capacity. Women may be appointed to office; they may become lobbyists, campaign managers, or members of elected officials' staffs.

Because what Americans call "politics" is so inclusive, we have devoted this book almost entirely to the story of women in elective office. A segment discusses volunteering, and one chapter covers nonelective political careers.

This book can only begin to explore the need for more women to represent us in America's town meetings, city councils, mayor's offices, county commissions, state legislatures, and the United States Congress. Women make up more than half the electorate, yet only a small proportion are elected officeholders.

Because of the considerable time needed to research this topic, write and edit the manuscript, and print the book, some of the women mentioned may no longer hold office, and new faces may have appeared on the political scene. Yet whether in office or not, we hope their stories will inspire you and the career details will prepare you for a future in politics.

Acknowledgments

Many people have helped in many ways to give life to this book. We are indeed grateful for their contributions and thank them all. Among the many are these, whose contributions are especially appreciated.

First and foremost, our thanks go to Karen Bennis, our indefatigable typist. She gave our manuscript all the translating skill and interpretive scholarship expended on the Dead Sea Scrolls—and it needed it! And thanks, also, to Elsa Scherphorn, who helped with the typing.

In addition, we wish to thank:

- Kirk Hoffmeier, librarian, Free Library of Philadelphia, for his assistance now and in the past in providing printouts of our subject area.
- Marie Wolcroft of the Wissahickon Library, Ambler, Pennsylvania, for all the interlibrary loan material she secured on our behalf.
- Trudy Buri, Adult Resources Librarian of Wissahickon Library, for cheerfully digging up research materials.
- Mary Ann Gabel, Republican Committeewoman of Montgomery County, Pennsylvania, for clarifying politics at the local level and for taking the time to read our manuscript; and Pennsylvania State Representatives Ruth Harper and Frances Weston for their insightful interviews.
- Bertina Groves, Millie L. Dancy, Marian Briceboyd, and Patsy Smith, Representative Harper's assistants; Linda Carrier and Nancy Garner, Representative Weston's legislative aides; and Mimi Lindelow and Marc Schuhl, staff aides to Pennsylvania

xii ACKNOWLEDGMENTS

State Representative Lois Hagarty, for helping with arrangements.
- John McCarthy of the Republican Information Office of the General Assembly of Pennsylvania for photographic assistance.
- Lucy Baruch of the Center for the American Woman in Politics, Eagleton Institute of Politics, Rutgers University, New Brunswick, New Jersey, for providing complete information about this unusual political resource.
- Carol Gisburne of C & G Stationers, Flourtown, Pennsylvania, for the unlikely but necessary combination of copy-making resources and political insights.
- Amy Denker, student at the Springside School, Philadelphia, for sharing her political workshop experiences with us.
- All the cooperative people connected with the General Assembly of the Commonwealth of Pennsylvania in Harrisburg, for helping us understand and report on young people in state government: Suzanne Bell, Director of Senate Pages; Jeannie Maley, Assistant to Director of Senate Pages; Ann Marie Otzel, Senate Page; Pennsylvania State Senators Jeanette F. Riebman, Eugene Scanlon, and John Shumaker; Mark Corrigan, Secretary of the Senate; Brian Foster, Photographer, Pennsylvania State Senate.
- Those who furnished material on political workshops: Marianne Alexander, PhD, Executive Director of Public Leadership Education Network, Goucher College, Towson, Maryland; Karen Papke, Assistant Director of the Congressional Seminar, Washington Workshops, Washington, DC; Eileen Hanning, Research Assistant, The Close Up Program, Washington, DC; the representatives of the Presidential Classroom and the Presidential Workshops; and Lawrence LeFebre, National Director, Voice of Democracy and Youth Activities of the Veterans of Foreign Wars.
- Dr. Jack Nagel, Associate Professor of Political Science, University of Pennsylvania, Philadelphia, for expanding our political horizons.
- Edna Manzer, PhD, Instructor in History, and Virginia Day, Head of the Middle School, Germantown Academy, Fort Washington, Pennsylvania, for their special contributions.

- Jeff Donaldson-Forbes, Assistant to the Publisher, The Rosen Publishing Group, for cheerful help on many levels.
- The bellmen at the Flanders Hotel, Ocean City, New Jersey, for their unfailing interest in the progress of each book we work on by the sea.
- Tim Bruno, owner of the Hoagie Stop, for allowing me to compose over a LONG cup of tea.
- And finally, a big thank-you to M.J. Fischer, neighbor and friend, whose pool and terrace gave us an unaccustomed ambiance in which to write.

We also wish to thank the Washington Workshops Foundation for permission to reprint in Chapter IV the comments by the junior high school and high school students concerning their Washington Workshop experiences.

Chapter **1**

Your Future in Politics

Did you know that a woman ran for President more than a hundred years ago? Belva Ann Lockwood, the first woman to plead a case before the Supreme Court of the United States, made a run for the country's top office in 1884. She was in fact the second woman to do so but the first to gain any electoral votes.

If she were here today, Belva Ann Lockwood would probably be surprised—and perhaps upset—to learn how few women have followed her into politics. She might be shocked to hear that women, who make up 55 percent of the population, are Neanderthals when it comes to representation. They hold barely 15 percent of the offices in state legislatures, city governments, and other political areas. You can count women governors on the fingers of one hand. Only two women serve in the U.S. Senate and only a few in the House of Representatives.

On the other hand, Mrs. Lockwood might be pleased to hear that women have made considerable advances in the last ten years. The number of women state legislators has almost tripled, and women are doing more political organizing than ever before, working to see that other women are elected.

Also, more women are entering politics earlier in their lives. It used to be that many women waited until their children were grown before tackling the heavy duty of running for public office. Not so today. In fact, some women are even planning to run for office as soon as they graduate from college. So we are bound to have more women in office because they are entering the field at every stage of adult life.

Running for office at a younger age has significance for you.

If you are thinking of a career in politics, you should know that you can formally enter the field as soon as you have finished your studies. And you can do a lot politically before you graduate.

In a different way, you can start political activity in junior high school. You can take a special interest in your history and government classes. You can sign up for the Washington Workshops political seminar described in Chapter IV. And you can participate in whatever form of student government your school offers.

In high school and college you can become politically knowledgeable in many ways. Civics or social science courses in high school and a political science major in college are valuable experiences. Attending more advanced political seminars, volunteering at a candidate's headquarters, and taking an interest in women's political issues are all ways to be active in politics early.

From your student vantage point, you may note that political attitudes toward women are changing for the better. Women candidates are no longer the exception. They now share political power equally with men in many areas. Presidential candidate Michael Dukakis chose a woman as his campaign manager in 1988. Nearly a quarter of the aides to U.S. Senators today are women. Increasing numbers of women are now running for office and winning posts as governors, mayors, and state legislators.

Women who run for office add quality to politics. They are valuable, knowledgeable, and often better qualified than men. The hard part is to convince the voters—women as well as men—that this is so.

In these pages you'll meet some of the American women who have convinced the voters that government and politics are not for men only. And who knows? One of these days, you may take your place beside them.

Chapter II

Politics Is Tough—but So Are Women!

As a woman politician, one of the things you must be able to accept is that politics is *tough*. While its rewards are great—serving your constituents, improving situations where you see need for improvement—the political arena is also stressful and sometimes unpleasantly revealing. Chapter III discusses the qualities you need to cope with an often hostile world.

Politics involves trade-offs. ("I'll help you get your bridge built if you'll vote for my day-care bill.") It also involves a strong tilt toward the male politician. Women can be competent and qualified, but if men have favors to return to other men, all the competence in the world won't give a woman the power or the position she may very well deserve.

Politics is a game, and a woman has to learn to play it. She can't be *above* politics or she'll be *out* of politics.

Women candidates and legislators experience sex discrimination at every turn. It is not as obvious as it once was, but it is there. It comes in questions like this one, addressed to a woman gubernatorial candidate and her female campaign manager: "Which one of you dames is running for governor?" Or it may be the oft-heard question, "How can you care for your children and still be a good legislator?" Or even in questions as silly as, "Why would a woman run against another woman in a campaign?" (Would a man ever ask another man, "Why are you running against a man?")

The Democratic and Republican parties are making efforts to include women in all parts of the political process. Men within the parties are beginning to realize that a woman's voice and a woman's vote have clout. They are now including women as a gesture of goodwill but also as part of a healthy concern for their own political futures. As an example, over 47 percent of the delegates to the 1988 Democratic National Convention were women. As you will read, however, the percentage of women in elective office—the heart and soul of American politics—is far below such a level.

A recent letter to columnist Walter Scott of *Parade* magazine concerned Elizabeth Dole, in 1989 named Secretary of Labor, and her possible qualifications for the Presidency. Scott's measured response shows that strong male-female stereotypes still exist. He wrote that Mrs. Dole was a gentle, educated, and agreeable person, but that these were not necessarily the right traits for a President. He went on to say that the office "...requires decisiveness, resolution, courage, calmness under fire, and intensive political experience." The clear implication was that Mrs. Dole lacked those characteristics.

Elizabeth Dole has been appointed to various political offices since the Presidency of Lyndon Baines Johnson in the 1960s. (Isn't twenty years in public service "intensive political experience"?) Mrs. Dole worked in President Johnson's Office of Consumer Affairs and during the Ford administration as a consumer advocate on the Federal Trade Commission. Michael Pertschuk, a former FTC chairman, says that whenever the Commission needed support Elizabeth Dole "was a real team fighter." That covers Scott's implied criticism that Dole is not a strong-willed, decisive person. In fact, White House staff people commented that she got one-tenth of everything she asked for on behalf of the FTC because she asked for everything. That sounds like a woman who could be persistent. Later, as head of the Department of Transportation, Elizabeth Dole fought to modernize services and provide more air traffic controllers.

Until more men are convinced that women have equal capabilities, women must make special efforts to help other women get into office. A woman who is elected or appointed to office is in an excellent position to bring other women into her official circle. These women in turn will be able to cite their experience as staff members as they build their political futures. As Carrie Saxon Perry, Mayor of Hartford, Connecticut, commented after she took the oath of office, "This place must be feminized." And she set about doing it.

As a black woman, Carrie Saxon Perry is a double-minority politician. Asked if she considered being black a handicap, she saw it rather as a plus. The "plus" was that she could be a role model to young black people and women. "I can be an example to young people. I tell them to put grades first, to make high grades a priority."

High grades and postgraduate degrees are not unusual for black female politicians. Members of these "double-whammy" groups, as Celinda Lake of the Women's Campaign Fund describes them, are overall more highly educated and more politically experienced than the average female politician. Many of them hold law degrees.

Nonetheless, the number of black women in politics is pitifully small. Cardiss Collins of Illinois is the only black woman serving in Congress; and of the 7,461 state legislators throughout the nation, only 91 are black women.

Barbara Jordan and Shirley Chisholm are two outstanding role models. Both served several terms in Congress after having been state legislators. Both continue to speak for blacks, for women, and against discrimination in the political arena.

Because of women like Jordan, Chisholm, and other vocal leaders, women are particularly successful at the state and local levels. Their words have inspired many to seek office who would otherwise have hesitated.

As Shirley Chisholm observed, women are the "backbone of American politics." Unfortunately, she meant that they were also in the back *rooms* of American politics! Women are the campaign letter-writers, envelope-stuffers, telephone-answerers. Their political talents are not being used; they stand on the sidelines of the game.

More women need the opportunity to be our elected officials. When women are considered serious candidates along with their male counterparts, America will have twice the talent pool to draw from.

That's what true democracy is all about!

Chapter **III**

The Woman Politician: Sugar and Spice

...but not necessarily nice. She has to be tough in a world that prepares men but not women to be leaders. She must be ready to trade verbal insults if necessary and fight for her beliefs.

At the same time, a woman politician may retain a pleasant, friendly demeanor. She can be womanly yet firm in her interaction with male colleagues.

As a student you may have these qualities—or be working on them. There are things you can do now that will prepare you for a political life later. If you participate in extracurricular activities —particularly in a leadership area such as student government— you will develop organizational skills and the ability to deal with people and to express yourself well. If you are an outgoing person who works well with other people, you will have a head start in the political game. You will have learned to "work the crowd" long before you register as a candidate.

In politics women are recognized for the hard workers they are. They serve as volunteers and run successful campaigns for male candidates, and male politicians staff their offices with dedicated women. Women must be willing to work harder than men. They are accustomed to being volunteers and are often more conscientious and more dedicated than men because they have to prove themselves in that way.

Mayor Perry of Hartford says that the average voter still has "...reservations about whether a woman can perform and excel." Because this doubt exists, women must be exceptional. Being exceptional means that the woman candidate must be:

- ambitious,
- hard-working,
- analytical,
- clear-thinking,
- farsighted,
- bold,
- energetic.

Sound like the Girl Scout Oath? Well, that's not all! A female politician must be able to withstand pressures that range from lack of privacy to surviving a primary race. If she is a state or national legislator, she has the added strain of being away from home for periods of time.

Along with an abundance of energy, Ms. Politician has to be tough. And one of the areas where she must display this toughness is in funding her campaigns.

As we will show more fully in Chapter VIII on campaigning for office, women traditionally do not like to ask for material things or favors. For instance, they don't like to ask for money. Particularly, money for *themselves*. It isn't "feminine," and it isn't the way they were brought up. But a woman has to ask for financial help for her campaign, or perish. She must learn to do it in an assertive, positive way. According to Mayor Sue Myrick of Charlotte, North Carolina, "[a lack of] money is the biggest deterrent to running for higher office." (The cost of a campaign for a U.S. House of Representatives seat may be well over $1 million; a Senate seat, up to $20 million!) And for most women most of the time the money simply isn't there. Men hold the political purse strings, and so far they're not willing to share.

If a woman must be tough about raising money, she must be aggressive when campaigning as well. A woman politician must ignore the criticisms and innuendos of her opponent. Many of these verbal darts are directed at women with families. A reporter will ask a female candidate, "Who will take care of the house while you're away on state business?" An opponent will ask a young mother/candidate, "Who will take care of the children?" No one would ask a man such questions. (On the other hand, when she ran for office, Senator Barbara Mikulski of Maryland, who is single, was criticized by her opponent for *not* having a family.)

These comments typify the sex discrimination that is practiced, and women must learn to counteract it. They must learn to return fire on the subtle put-downs and not be discouraged from running for office. A woman should not wait to be asked to run for office. Men may call her pushy, but that is simply a weapon to discourage her. "No one hands over power. You have to take it," says Ann Lewis, political director of Americans for Democratic Action. "Be bold," says Jane Campbell, an Ohio State Representative. "Politics is now a career. You look at the top of an organization and consider how you might get there."

That is indeed what a farsighted politician must do. And she will do it better if she accepts Madeleine Kunin's estimate of female politics. Kunin, Governor of Vermont, says: "There is something very hostile about politics. It is not behavior women are brought up to do."

According to Jeane Kirkpatrick, former U.S. Ambassador to the United Nations, "...those [male legislators] who are lawyers have practice in adversary proceedings," which means that they are more at home with the conflict that is part of politics. But Kirkpatrick also believes that many women consider politics more in terms of public service than of conflict. About the women legislators she interviewed for her book *Political Woman,* Kirkpatrick wrote: "None of these women thinks of government as principally concerned with compromising or policing. All describe government in terms of solving problems and achieving progress." Kirkpatrick concluded that these women demonstrated their ability to handle conflict by the very fact that they had survived the rigors of campaigning. (See Chapter V for more about women and the conflicts of politics.)

Ellen Malcolm, President of EMILY, holds that every female politician must be thick-skinned and ready for the fray. She can win if she doesn't let name-calling and petty accusations get to her—and *women* opponents can sling mud, too! (EMILY, incidentally, stands for Early Money Is Like Yeast, and is a fund that supports certain women politicians. Many a successful candidate owes her political victory at least in part to EMILY campaign funds.)

This boldness, this toughness, will lead a woman politician to do her best work. It will enable her to stand alone for an unpopular but worthwhile cause. Effective women politicians will often display an independent spirit even as they wear their party's label.

Chapter **IV**

Junior High and High School

Even if you are in junior high, you have probably become interested in local and national political races. Your parents may talk politics, and you have probably followed the political scene on radio and television.

Politics is part of your school day, too. Your Social Science and Problems of Democracy classes focus on local and national government. If you are a class officer or active in clubs you have a chance to develop leadership qualities.

Another way to become familiar with politics is to sign up for the junior high program promoted by the Washington Workshops Foundation (3222 N Street NW, Washington, DC 20007). The program consists of week-long seminars that are held from February through June each year and are open to 7th, 8th and 9th graders.

The Foundation's program offers exciting political experience and an opportunity to tour Washington landmarks. Typical days begin with visits to Capitol Hill and discussions with congressional staff assistants. Afternoons are filled with discussions of the morning's events, followed by tours of the city. The week's activities also include free time for sports activities and indoor swimming.

The Issues Debate on Friday evening caps the week's activities. This session is prepared by the students themselves. Boys and girls plan an agenda designed to spark heated political debate.

Students nationwide have enjoyed their junior high experience in Washington. A participant from Dix Hills, New York, noted: "It was our Easter vacation and...I said: 'I hope this is going to be good because I'm sacrificing my vacation.' Now that the [sem-

12   CAREERS FOR WOMEN IN POLITICS

COURTESY WASHINGTON WORKSHOPS FOUNDATION
Junior high school students attend an event on the South Lawn of the White House.

inar] week is over, it was no sacrifice—it was beautiful, one of the best vacations I ever had."

A student from Lancaster, Pennsylvania, wrote: "It was a tremendous experience to meet with such an outstanding group of lads from all over... I want to thank you all for the things I learned, and for making us feel like a family. I've made friends I'll treasure always because of this."

High school also provides rich seminar experiences, and it offers an even greater opportunity to prepare for a political career. As a female high school student you can make your career choice now. Only recently have women students been able to consider a practical future in politics, but female role models and media coverage now make politics a more viable career.

If you plan to go into politics, you can take courses in high school that will familiarize you with the political process. Civics and social studies courses will help you learn how government operates. History, government, and current events courses will pay off in political knowledge when you become an active campaigner.

Even math, business courses, sociology, and other subjects are helpful because politics is all-encompassing. It involves an understanding of people, a knowledge of society, and administrative skills. Thus, every course becomes a plus. Even sports has its place; regular exercise keeps you in shape for the rigors of a political race.

Extracurricular activities such as student council and debating will give you opportunities to acquire leadership skills. If you can get up on a stage and run an event on current affairs, you are really understudying for future political activity. You'll probably develop the knack for bargaining that is so much a part of politics: "Hey, guys, if you'll vote to bring the prom back to the gym this year, I'll support your hoagie sales campaign for band uniforms!"

Back in the early 1960s, one teenage student, Melody Miller, became interested in political activity. Melody had become interested in President John F. Kennedy and inspired by his vision of the country's future. After school hours she worked at the Democratic Party offices, became involved in the Young Democrats organization, and worked part time in a congressional office.

But it was through the unlikely setting of an art class that Melody Miller met her destiny. In her senior year she sculpted a bust of President Kennedy, only to have it crack when it was fired in the kiln. Undaunted, Melody glued the sculpture together and entered it in her school's art show.

The father of another student was a newspaper reporter. He was told about Melody's efforts as he toured the art show. Impressed by her tenacity, he wrote a short article on the broken bust.

The story was read by a White House aide, who sent it along to Evelyn Lincoln, President Kennedy's secretary. Mrs. Lincoln told the President about it, and he decided to meet his young admirer. Melody received a message in class the next day that the President would like to see her. The meeting led to the President's inviting Melody to work on his 1964 campaign.

There *was* no 1964 campaign for President Kennedy. His assassination ended Melody's dream and the dreams of many others. But during college and in the twenty years that followed Ms. Miller continued to work for the Kennedy family, first for Robert and then for Ted.

Melody Miller is still at the White House, as deputy press secre-

14   CAREERS FOR WOMEN IN POLITICS

COURTESY WASHINGTON WORKSHOPS FOUNDATION
Supreme Court Justice Sandra Day O'Connor discusses the courts and the Constitution before a teenage seminar.

tary and spokesperson. And she is still excited about politics. She enjoys the power her position offers and the thrill of working where historic events have taken place.

Ms. Miller is just one of many who have felt the pull of politics while still in school. Other students can participate in other ways. Anne Marie Otzel, for example, took advantage of an opportunity open to many young people: She became a legislative page.

Serving as a page is an excellent way to get acquainted with politics while in high school. The U.S. Senate and the House of Representatives have positions for pages, or messengers, to serve the legislators from their respective states. Many state legislatures do, too. If you're interested in serving in Washington, write to the local offices of your U.S. Senators, or your area's Representative. Do the same for your state legislators if you live near your state capital.

Anne Marie is fortunate: She lives in Harrisburg, the capital of Pennsylvania. As a senior at Central Dauphin East High School, she attends school in the mornings and serves as a State Senate page each afternoon. Her job, one of the school's many co-op opportunities, earns her three credits toward graduation.

Ann Marie has a super boss, Suzanne Bell, Senate Page Director, who oversees Ann Marie and other high school and college students. A role model herself, Mrs. Bell is the first woman to serve in an executive position in the Pennsylvania legislature.

When Ann Marie is called to the Senate floor, she sits on one of two long benches near the rostrum at the front of the chamber. The Senate chamber, with its impressive traditional architecture and murals of George Washington, Benjamin Franklin, Abraham Lincoln, and others, is a fitting background for the state's official business.

The Pennsylvania Senate upholds an interesting tradition. Pages and Senators may not cross an imaginary line in the center of the aisle that divides the Democratic and Republican sides of the chamber. If Ann Marie is serving the Democratic side for the day, she must observe protocol in delivering a Democratic Senator's message to the Republican side by handing it to a Republican page, who then takes it to the person for whom it is intended.

This type of errand is what Senate pages mostly do. The page's duty off the floor involves taking documents and messages to Senators and staff within the Capitol as well as to state offices in nearby buildings.

As this is written, Ann Marie is not sure about her future. She likes the excitement of being a Senate page, but psychology is also an interest of hers. During a recent summer she volunteered in the psychatric wing of a hospital. In politics, it pays to have diverse interests. Ann Marie may some day serve her state in an official way, her work complemented by a background in psychology. Any politician will readily admit that a psychology background would help in understanding the wishes of the voters and the attitudes of fellow legislators!

Many other opportunities are available to experience practical politics while you are still in high school. One is the Presidential Classroom sponsored by *Newsweek* magazine. The Presidential Classroom hosts eight one-week sessions in Washington for high school juniors and seniors. During these weeks students from all

16   CAREERS FOR WOMEN IN POLITICS

BRIAN FOSTER PHOTO

Senate Page Ann Marie Otzel receives an assignment from Mark Corrigan, Secretary of the Pennsylvania Senate.

over the United States attend congressional hearings, seminars, and lectures given by government experts. They can also meet with their Senator or Representative, or one of their aides.

The seminars focus on such issues as lobbying and the effect of the media on policy and national defense strategies. Students are encouraged to give their own opinions and conclusions on topics that concern the Congress and the Executive branch of government. Students also visit landmarks of the city, attend a dinner theater, and make friends with some of the other four hundred students attending each session.

If you are interested in attending a Presidental Classroom, check with your school adviser at the beginning of the school year, or write Presidential Classroom, 441 North Lee Street, Alexandria, VA 22314. The programs, held from January to June of each year, are open to students in the top 25 percent of their class and having a B+ average. Students must also have a solid record of extra-curricular activity and be approved by their school's principal.

One student who attended a recent program was well pleased with the experience. Amy Denker, President of Student Government at Springside School in suburban Philadelphia, found it generally worthwhile. "It was less academic than I expected and more fun," commented Amy. She found most of the seminars and speakers stimulating. Some congressional committee hearings were exciting because of the drama of current issues. "It was fascinating just to be able to walk into a hearing and watch how national and international decisions are made," she noted.

What Amy Denker noticed particularly was the delegation of power. Congressional aides do a great deal of official paperwork and are a strong force behind the legislature. This is the only way a legislator can get things done.

Amy has found a similar need to delegate power as she leads Student Government. "My role is as a facilitator," she explains. "I delegate tasks to other students, and this way everything gets done."

Amy already appears to have the personality for politics. She's involved, interested, and caring. But does she really want to go into politics? "It's obviously exhausting, but appealing." She feels there's not much room for one's own life. "Your life is circumscribed." Also, her idealism, gained from American History courses, is compromised by the political corruption she sees. "Still," she says, "I like the power and energy of politics." It seems likely that Amy Denker will head toward public office one day, armed with her enthusiasm and her activist qualities.

The Close Up Program (Close Up Foundation, 1235 Jefferson Davis Highway, Arlington, VA 22202) is another week-long seminar based in Washington DC at which 10th, 11th and 12th graders throughout the country learn firsthand how their country is governed.

Close Up has no grade-average requirement. Although the seminar can take a large bite out of the family budget, fellowships are available for those whose families meet eligibility guidelines.

Close Up participants visit Congress and sit in on hearings. They have opportunities to question administration officials, lobbyists, and policymakers.

Close Up encourages students to evaluate what they hear and to report on their impressions. The week's seminars may run the political gamut from the role of the Supreme Court to Pentagon activities. A recent forum included a talk on women in politics.

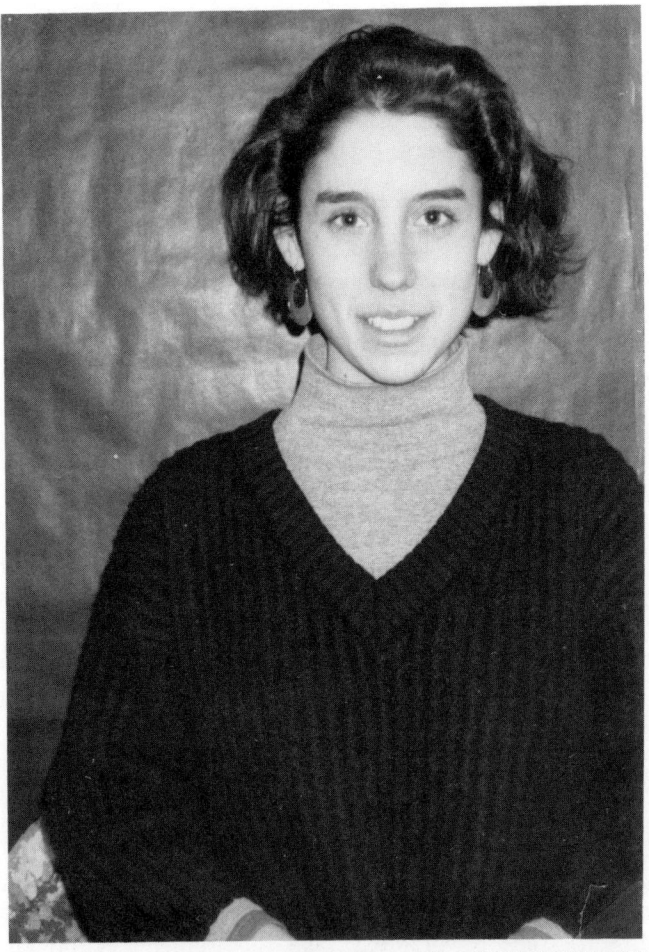

COURTESY SPRINGSIDE SCHOOL

Amy Denker, a student at the Springside School, Philadelphia, and an attendee at a Presidential Classroom seminar in Washington, DC.

A typical teacher in the Close Up program is David Bailor, who uses the streets of Washington as his classroom. He gives his students a new understanding of their role as U.S. citizens as they tour the buildings and monuments they've known only through history texts.

The Congressional Seminar, sponsored by the Washington

Workshops Foundation, is another political experience for high school students. The Seminar is aimed at "...teenage Americans who will assume their voting rights...and go on to adulthood and positions of leadership in an America of the 21st century."

With this in mind, the Washington Workshop plans seminars for our future leaders. These include meetings with the Senate Committee on Commerce, Science and Transportation and the Committee on Foreign Relations, and the House Select Committee on Narcotics Abuse and Control. Committee decisions on these subjects and others help determine our future role nationally and internationally.

High school students have an opportunity to attend House and Senate sessions and meet with members of the White House staff. Their daytime experiences lead to lively evenings spent developing a "Model Congress," with students forming committees to draft legislation. At the Friday session the Model Congress meets and votes for final legislation under traditional House rules. Debate before the final vote is always spirited. The students enjoy putting together a minigovernment and running it.

Congressional Seminar students are encouraged to pursue any specific political interest they may have. If students take this opportunity, they enrich themselves as well as the Workshops.

The Washington Workshops Foundation allows plenty of time for sightseeing and informal activities. Home base for visiting students is the beautiful Marymount University in Arlington, Virginia. Those heading for college will have an advance taste of campus life.

Students from recent Congressional Seminars have been delighted with their experiences. Said Chris Falkenberry of Scarsdale High School, Scarsdale, New York: "I have recently returned from Congressional Seminar #8, and I am hard pressed to remember another week in which I had such a great time. The program was excellent. Every aspect of the program impressed me, from the caliber of the people to the list of important speakers and the professionalism of the staff. I arrived in Washington a bit overwhelmed by the complexity of the government. As students, we are very lucky that organizations such as this one exist. I hope more people are able to take advantage of your fantastic program."

COURTESY WASHINGTON WORKSHOPS FOUNDATION

Washington Workshops participants question Senator Mitch McConnell (R-Ky) on issues of the day

Howard Kirkland from Loudon High School, Loudon, Tennessee, commented: "Never before have I been made so aware of the issues that confront our nation. I congratulate you on being able to organize such an interesting, informative, and fun program....Please continue to keep up the quality, professionalism, and excellence of the learning environment which exists at the Washington Workshops' Congressional Seminars."

Another way for students to express themselves on government issues is the Veterans of Foreign Wars Voice of Democracy contest. (Voice of Democracy, V.F.W. National Headquarters, Broadway at 34th Street, Kansas City, MO 64111.) The Voice of Democracy is a broadcast scriptwriting scholarship program offered through every high school in the country. Tenth through 12th grade students are eligible to compete for generous scholarships to the college of their choice. The winners also have an opportunity to visit Washington.

The contest assignment is for students, individually or as a class, to create a three- to five-minute broadcast tape on a theme relevant to democracy. The theme differs from year to year; in a recent year it was "America's Liberty—Our Heritage." Each student tape is judged on originality, content, and the quality of the delivery of the message. Originality as defined by the V.F.W. is a positive, imaginative approach. The contest entry needs to be logical, clear, and concise. Sincerity, pronunciation, and expressiveness are the key factors of a well-delivered speech.

Local V.F.W. chapters sponsor the high school competitions in their area. The winner from each high school goes on to compete at the state level. The state winner then faces the winners from the other 49 states. Each state winner is awarded a five-day, all-expense-paid trip to the nation's capital and a chance to compete for scholarship money.

In addition to the political programs for high school students, one is offered for high school teachers. It is designed to help them teach young women to think positively about themselves. It should be no surprise that this target program was developed at a women's college, Wellesley College, in Wellesley, Massachusetts.

Teachers from various parts of the country attend special classes and come away with new understandings about contemporary women, which they in turn share with other high school teachers. These new understandings are then presented to students with across-the-board curriculum changes.

Every subject from history to chemistry is "double-gendered." Prominent women in history are considered along with their male counterparts. Perceptions held by women may also be considered. For instance, a course on contemporary politics might pose the question: Do women define politics differently from men? If this is the case—and, as this book shows, it often is—high school girls should certainly be aware of those differences. Knowing about them may make it easier for young women if they should decide on political careers.

Dr. Edna Manzer, a history teacher at Germantown Academy in Fort Washington, Pennsylvania, was one of those chosen by the Wellesley College program to instruct other teachers in young women's consciousness-raising. She also emphasizes both male and female contributions in all her own classes.

One course Mrs. Manzer particularly enjoys teaching is Gender and Identity. The students learn about female roles today and how confusing they can be to both men and women. Women students learn to value their own unique qualities and reach for opportunities based on those qualities. At the same time, they are taught how to achieve goals without a shrill attack on traditional fortresses. Men react positively to a low-key, reasoned approach from women, Dr. Manzer maintains.

Boys often elect to take Dr. Manzer's course. They, too, learn to rethink the so-called accepted roles of women in society.

Chapter **V**

College

If you're headed for a political career, you can get a thorough grounding in the field at junior or community colleges and at four-year colleges and universities.

Montgomery County Community College, outside of Philadelphia, has a challenging series of political courses. Students can begin with an introduction to political science, which provides a set of "reference tools" including a background in political systems and institutions and political behavior.

Because community colleges are often a transfer point to the final two years of a four-year college, it seems worthwhile to describe the political science courses offered by Montgomery County Community College. These would be taken along with other courses required for graduation with an Associate Degree in Political Science.

POL 102 is an examination of the American government. The interplay between Congress, the President, and the judicial branch is part of the focus, as well as a study of political parties, pressure groups, and lobbyists.

POL 110 researches state and local government. The course is primarily concerned with the many powers of local government. Every state legislature and county governing body has the power to tax its citizens, enforce laws, and promote social and economic welfare. The latter powers would be particularly interesting to the future woman politician because social and economic changes are often at the heart of her platform.

POL 115 and POL 117 study constitutional law. It concentrates on how the U.S. Constitution governs Supreme Court decisions. After more than two hundred years, this document remains the most powerful directive in American government. Because the Executive branch (the President) appoints Supreme Court Justices —subject to the consent of the Senate—the Court's interpretation of the Constitution may swing from liberal to conservative depending on the viewpoints of the Justices appointed by various administrations. Many Supreme Court cases involve issues of particular interest to women: pro-life versus pro-choice, equal pay, and inequities in the workplace. So a full understanding of how the Court operates is essential to the woman planning to take part in American politics.

Another course focuses on comparative government, on other countries' political systems, and on international organizations such as the Common Market and the NATO alliance.

Another course with a world overview concentrates on international politics in the 20th century. The curriculum includes a study of war, nationalism, imperialism, and diplomatic relations. An in-depth study of these problems can make the student a better judge of media reportage. Television, radio, newspapers, and news magazines report on political and diplomatic activities thousands of miles away from us—not always without a viewpoint of their own. By knowing the international territory, the student can interpret these events for herself.

The college also offers two government internship programs for political science majors. Each course involves 15 hours of classroom work and 120 hours of political field experience. The student seeking an internship must find a government institution to sponsor him or her. Such a student might be fortunate enough to work as an aide to a state representative, a state senator, a mayor, or other regional officeholder.

Four-year colleges and universities offer more extensive programs than the two-year college. The student majoring in political science at most colleges will be so familiar with the political process by graduation that she will be prepared when she steps out on her own.

The University of Pennsylvania, in Philadelphia, has an impressive political science curriculum. Among its approaches to a political science degree is the opportunity to earn bachelor's and master's degrees concurrently. Students with one or more political science degrees gain a unique perspective on their subject.

This perspective comes from professors such as Dr. Jack Nagel, who endow their courses with far more than facts and political theory. Teachers like Dr. Nagel are scientists—political scientists—and they see politics and government from a psychologically complete yet objective point of view. As scientists, they can stand back from their subject; as teachers, they can enable the students to make decisions based on detailed political analysis.

In an interview, Dr. Nagel outlined a possible curriculum and offered an enlightening view of practical politics.

His advice on a course of study for women affirms his general theories about politics. He suggests basic courses in political science and government. He believes that students should have a thorough grounding in our government's history in order to make sound political decisions. History provides insight because new national and global problems can be viewed in light of earlier events.

The "standard" political science courses at the University are augmented by some intriguing, offbeat ones. Dr. Nagel teaches Politics as a Practical Art, a course that can help women handle a rather abrasive world if they choose politics. He points out that conflict is inevitable in politics. Women have been brought up to shy away from confrontation, preferring to settle problems through reason and cooperation. Idealism and cooperation are fine character traits, Dr. Nagel contends, but women must face conflict in politics as a fact of life. Democracy has a checks-and-balances system: It guarantees that what makes one group happy will displease another. Thus conflict is built into the system. If women do not take it personally, but look at the system practically, they will see that *positive* conflict can produce better government.

Political Participation, another of Dr. Nagel's courses, points up the passiveness of today's voters and political volunteers. The immensity and confusion of our democratic system of government makes us political fence-sitters; we sit it out rather than sort it out. We need to be motivated, to have a strong sense of obligation. Our freedom is making us free to do nothing—particularly on Election Day.

Dr. Nagel also notes that fewer people work to help candidates get elected, resulting in weaker political parties. The decline in helping hands is because our patronage system is weakening.

Patronage—a word once equated with corruption and still not disassociated from it—is defined as returning favor for favor. You help me win an election and I'll get you a job in my administration. And, surprisingly, it does work! One is motivated to elect a candidate because there's a guaranteed return—a job or a favor if he or she wins. Because the patronage system is no longer as strong as it was in the days of Tammany Hall, fewer people are interested in working for something that benefits them only indirectly.

Other courses that Dr. Nagel believes would be helpful to women (and men) include Social Psychology and Group Dynamics. These courses, taught in the Psychology Department, affirm that political action occurs in a group situation and that attitudes play a strong role in public office. It is important to know which attitudes work for positive action.

Finally, for women specifically, Dr. Nagel suggests taking Women's Studies programs, including Sex and Sexism, Sociology of Gender, and Discrimination. These and other Women's Study courses are designed to make women more politically self-assured.

Those majoring in Political Science at the university may be invited to join the National Political Science Honor Society, Pi Sigma Alpha. There is also a Political Science Student Committee on Undergraduate Education, which allows students to participate in curriculum development. This flexibility lets women propose subject areas that might help their political future.

Dr. Nagel believes that the course activity program outlined here will launch a woman candidate—or at least will give her some solid training. But he also holds that there are four reasons why women are hindered when they seek political posts. We have already discussed the drawback of conflict. The other three problems are not solved through courses of study. One has to do with the woman's role as childbearer. Women generally have children in the years that are vital to building a political base. Therefore, many of them get into politics too late, or not at all. However, because women with young children are starting political careers earlier (and some are choosing not to have children), female representation will be greater at every level of government.

The third roadblock is nonsexist, although it may appear otherwise at first glance. Our democratic system is set up to discourage women from serving in office. This fact, Dr. Nagel explains, is not due to male interference. It is rather a problem of the complexity of the system. Dr. Nagel says: "In many other countries, party leaders, often women, will set up a balanced slate so that women can run for office. Local representation is so uncluttered that voters do not look through a bureaucratic thicket to find their candidates. In America the political system is so decentralized that no one has power over a central slate to ensure the population's wishes." In short, we may *want* women in office, but we've built a rat's maze to keep them from getting in.

Finally, there is the gender lag. Women have always been slow to get on the political bandwagon. America has been politically male-dominated since its inception; women earned the right to vote only in this century. Only now are we becoming "socialized equally," Dr. Nagel points out. And because of this lag, it will not be until near the middle of the 21st century that we can hope to close that gap.

Women must recognize the handicaps described by Dr. Nagel. But new awareness of their ability to make a difference can help offset these negatives. A good college education is one answer to turning this new perception of feminine power into political reality.

Several colleges now have women-in-politics programs established by PLEN, the Public Leadership Education Network, an organization supported in part by the Carnegie Foundation.

PLEN oversees existing women's leadership programs and encourages nonparticipating colleges to adopt the PLEN model. In establishing new bases, PLEN hopes to make college women politically educated and motivated.

The ten colleges currently offering the PLEN program are: Alverno College, Milwaukee, Wisconsin; Carlow College, Pittsburgh, Pennsylvania; The College of St. Catherine, St. Paul, Minnesota; Douglass College, The Women's College of Rutgers University, New Brunswick, New Jersey; Goucher College, Towson, Maryland; Marymount Manhattan College, New York, New York; Mount Vernon College, Washington, D.C.; Spelman College, Atlanta, Georgia; Stephens College, Columbia, Missouri; and Wells College, Aurora, New York.

Alverno College has chosen to develop a program of urban education to enlighten women students politically. The program examines women as policymakers and as urban dwellers. Students have the further opportunity of applying for urban policy internships.

At the College of St. Catherine students may choose courses that bring out their leadership abilities. Courses such as Communications Skills, Public Leadership Skills, and Personal Issues for Achieving Women give women students "net worth" leadership and other skills that otherwise might be gained only after years in politics.

Students at Douglass College benefit from proximity to Rutgers's Center for the American Woman and Politics. This Center, part of the Eagleton Institute of Politics, serves women politicians throughout the United States. They turn to the Center for counsel and meet within its walls to exchange ideas and shape policy.

Douglass College also has its share of women public leaders. The course Women and Politics has brought together women in three fields of expertise: those in elective office, appointive officeholders, and representatives of special-interest groups. The students are stimulated by the presence of these women in the forefront of politics.

The College also offers concrete ways for students to become involved. Visits to the state capital at Trenton and voter registration drives take college instruction out of the classroom.

Marymount Manhattan College has a study program that concentrates on one large policy area, human rights or the status of women. New York City, of course, has an abundance of resources for any political area under consideration.

Spelman College has several courses that focus on the role of black women in American leadership. Spelman has also adopted a visiting politician program that brings to the campus various black leaders as positive role models.

Wells College has established a politician-in-residence program for its women students. These politician-lecturers are a course-experience in themselves, sharing their expertise and helping the students plan leadership programs.

The programs just described are only a small part of the PLEN-based women-in-politics curricula these colleges offer. Write to the colleges mentioned for further information on their programs.

Several of the women's colleges mentioned offer public leadership internships. Many of these off-campus experiences turn out to be entrées into the world of politics. The work—from serving as legislative aide to hitting the campaign trail—may lead to full-time employment after graduation. Interns learn to research an issue, observe the actions of at least one politician at a public event, and perhaps even substitute at a meeting for an official who cannot attend.

College seminars also offer political experiences. One of the most prominent is the Washington Workshops' Advanced Congressional Seminar. It is open only to high school graduates and college students and consists of a three-week internship on Capitol Hill. Students work in congressional offices and make staff contacts that one day may well be valuable. In most cases, students work for a Senator or Representative from their home state.

The second segment of the Advanced Congressional Seminar is a required research project. A student may study the House of Representatives procedural rules, research a specific political issue, or acquire a detailed understanding of the legislative process. The Seminar awards three college credits and gives the student a comfortable political footing.

The Presidential Classroom has college as well as high school programs. Its Federal Forum is open to college students as well as administrators, government employees, and alumni of the Presidential Classroom.

The activities include discussions with Capitol Hill leaders and lobbyists, a look at current legislation on the congressional agenda, and receptions with foreign diplomats. The various activities end with a cruise down the Potomac River. Although the Federal Forum offers no college credit, it is an excellent introduction to national politics.

One college seminar designed exclusively for women is the Women in Public Policy Seminar. Sponsored by the National Women's Education Fund under the direction of PLEN, the seminar takes place each January. Like all PLEN activities, it is designed to educate women for public leadership. It is one thing to give young women an awareness of a gender imbalance, quite another to try to change it.

This seminar places its participants briefly in the national seat of government and asks them to participate in its activities. Women leaders from many political areas address the students. Recent speakers have included: The Honorable Sandra Day O'Connor, Associate Justice of the U.S. Supreme Court; Patricia Price Bailey, Commissioner, Federal Trade Commission; The Honorable Gladys Kessler, Judge of the District of Columbia Superior Court; and Martha Mautner, Deputy Director, Office of Eastern European and Soviet Union Affairs, Department of State.

From these and other distinguished women lecturers, seminar students learn how public policy affects women.

Attendees can earn three college credits. The Women in Public Policy Seminar includes a minimum of 45 hours of formal instruction, or "contact hours." It may be a turning point for a college student trying to make a career decision.

Majoring in political science is an obvious and rewarding way to familiarize yourself with the world of politics. But there are many other avenues to public service, and women politicians have used them all.

Other—although less direct—approaches to a political career are teaching and nursing. These fields offer opportunities to interact with people. A good "people person" can often be an effective politician.

Specific courses or areas can help political aspirants build their skills. Among these are courses in management, accounting, psychology, and computer science (computer literacy is essential for effective communication and campaign management in the fast-paced 1990s).

One political route that can help women compete on equal terms with men is the law. A college graduate in political science or pre-law who earns a law degree has a tremendous political advantage. (Many male politicians are or were lawyers.) This is because a law school graduate has learned the fine art of confrontation. (This point was mentioned earlier, but it belongs here in academic preparation, too.)

One woman legislator commented, "If you are a woman and a lawyer, you have an instant credibility that most women do not have." That is because much of government and policymaking parallels the law, with its presentation of two sides of an argument and its often adversarial, persuasive nature. The law involves a decision-making process not unlike that of government. Lawyers have their clients; legislators, their constituents. In each case, the job is to represent the interests of those you serve and to put down the opposition. (Of course, our legislators also seek consensus or agreement; otherwise, there would be no government.)

A woman with a law degree, then, can almost write her own ticket. But "almost" is the operative word. Her legal credentials —and her added credibility—may make it slightly easier for her to be victorious over a male opponent than she might be otherwise.

While college offers on-campus opportunities to work in politics (college students often become deeply involved in Presidential campaigns), opportunities also exist in the community to work for candidates and causes. For example, Teenage Young Republicans (ages seventeen to twenty-one) and Young Republicans (men and women in their twenties) manage to have fun and support their party, too. The Young Republicans of Montgomery County, Pennsylvania, have restaurant meetings with county commissioners to discuss campaign strategy. Young Republicans in this suburban township, as in others, do the "small potatoes" work political parties need. They stuff envelopes, campaign door-to-door, and serve as "gofers" on election days.

Mimi Lindelow, a Young Republican and legislative aide to Pennsylvania State Representative Lois Hagarty, suggests that anyone wishing to start a Young Republican group can talk to the staff at the nearest Republican Party headquarters. They will be able to tell you whether there is a chapter nearby, and if not, how to start one.

Young Democrats are equally active in many parts of the country. Local Democratic Party headquarters will have information on the organization's activities.

Eleanor Smeal, head of the Fund for the Feminist Majority, is looking for women candidates on college campuses these days. She believes that women must get into politics early and run often. They must move into the field when they are young because the top political prizes are won only after years in the field. Smeal says that college women are ready for politics. The question is: Is politics ready for *them*? The answer will be "yes" if enough college women consider politics as a serious career.

Stephanie Solein, former Executive Director of the Women's Campaign Fund, is another proponent of the start-early school. In the book *Momentum: Women in American Politics*, Solein says, "We have to identify women who are in this for the long haul. We don't need any more flashes in the pan. We need women who understand that if they are going to be taken seriously in politics and they are going to be successful they've got to get into it and make it a career and chart their course."

College, then, is a precious opportunity to start charting that course.

Chapter **VI**

Financial Resources for Political Study

It is possible to study politics, political science, and government at nearly any undergraduate college in the United States. Many colleges offer scholarships in those subjects.

Where do you find such scholarships? College catalogs are one source of detailed information, but a basic scholarship reference is your best starting point. Such a reference can also give you information about organizations that grant scholarships. The American Legion, for example, is one of the more generous scholarship funding organizations.

Probably the most comprehensive book of this kind is *Financial Aid for Higher Education* by Oreon Keesler. The reference section of your library may have it. Its Dewey Decimal System number is:

378.34
K258F4

You can find the type of scholarship program you want by checking such categories as government, government service, politics, and political science.

The United States Youth Program scholarship program is excellent for high school students. It offers a seminar similar to those described in the chapter on high school preparation for politics—except that in addition it includes a $15,000 William Randolph Hearst Foundation scholarship to the college you select. To be eligible, you must be a high school junior or senior who holds class office and demonstrates qualities of leadership. For details, write to Rita Almon, Director, United States Youth Program, 690 Market Street, San Francisco, CA 94104.

Among the many graduate schools available for the study of American politics and government is the Eagleton Institute of Politics at Rutgers, the State University of New Jersey. The Institute offers a one-year graduate Fellowship in Politics and Public Policy, leading to a Master of Arts in Political Science. The tightly structured curriculum includes a high level of interaction with faculty in small classes, and, to quote Rutgers: "...is designed to help students develop...a thorough understanding of the political processes and institutions through which public policies are formulated and implemented." Eagleton graduates are "...capable of conducting analysis and working effectively as or with elected officials and senior administrators."

Only fifteen to twenty Fellowships are awarded each year. They are open to women as well as men, but there is an added dimension: One of the three Eagleton centers devoted to public service and research is the Eagleton Center for the American Woman and Politics, which is one of America's outstanding research and information centers concerned with the historical and contemporary activities of women in the American political process.

Each semester Eagleton Fellowship recipients take required courses in public policy, in which they analyze the legislative history and administration of a federally funded program. Alternatively, they may conduct a research project on an issue of concern to state government officials. At the Eagleton Seminars, which are held regularly, they examine principal state and local election activities and follow the activities of local political party organizations. Well-known political figures including former President Gerald R. Ford have been among the many guest lecturers at the Eagleton Seminars.

Elective courses may be on the legislative process, the mass media, the Congress of the United States, women in politics, or elections and campaigning.

The Eagleton Institute was founded in 1957 and has graduated more than 400 political science candidates, many of whom have made notable contributions to American politics in elective and appointive positions.

White House Fellowships are for college graduates who are in the "early or formative years of career or profession." From fourteen to twenty of these Fellowships are offered each year by the federal government.

White House Fellows are assigned for one year of work with Presidential assistants in Cabinet-level agencies. They receive financial support during the internship year.

Selection is based on demonstrated leadership in community affairs. For more information, write to the President's Commission on White House Fellowships, P.O. Box 7737, Washington, DC 20044.

Once you are established in a politically related career, you are eligible for the ultimate program: an APSA Congressional Fellowship.

The American Political Science Association (APSA) was founded in 1903. With a membership of over 12,000, it is the major professional association for those who are active in American politics. You may someday benefit from its Fellowship Program if you become (1) a political professional, (2) a journalist concentrating on politics, or (3) a federal executive or a medical professional concerned with the federal government and health care. Women are qualifying in one of these areas in increasing numbers.

The Fellowship Program is designed "...to improve the quality of scholarship and teaching on [the workings of] Congress and American national politics; to enhance public understanding of Congress and policymaking; and to provide professionals...with practical experience in Congress and insight into the legislative process," according to the Association.

The program involves nearly a year of study and work. A month-long orientation provides intensive indoctrination in the workings of both houses of Congress. Fellows then work in congressional offices or on congressional committees. In this environment the officials and the Fellows teach each other a great deal from their different perspectives on government. A visit to the home territory of the Senator or Representative for whom the Fellow is working is usually part of the program.

In mid-April the Fellows who have been working in the House of Representatives change places with those at work in the Senate. This gives each Fellow a chance to see the differences between the two legislative bodies. For several weeks each spring a group also participates in an exchange program with their counterparts from Canada.

Chapter **VII**

Fighting the Myths and Considering a Run

Men put up barriers to keep women from running for office. *Women* put up barriers to keep women from office. Between male ingrained resistance to women candidates and women's insecurity about running, it is surprising that women are represented in office at all.

Three reasons come quickly to mind when we consider women's lack of representation in government. First, women like to be asked to do things. In politics you don't wait to be asked—you must leap into the fray and hold your banner high. Second, many women simply are not interested in politics; their childhood did not prepare them for the role, and their adult years may be occupied by myriad nonpolitical activities such as raising a family, serving on the PTA, and performing volunteer work.

Last, women don't believe that they can have a family and face the demands of politics at the same time. A politician's life is decidedly hectic. It includes unexpected emergency calls and constant travel from home whether a woman serves in the state legislature or at the national level.

Yes, a political role is demanding, but women *can* do it. Families tend to rally around a wife and mother in office. This support helps her to meet the many demands of her daily life.

In her book *Why and How Women Will Elect the Next President*, Eleanor Smeal, former president of NOW, discusses the many myths about why women shouldn't run for office. These myths, accepted as truths, discourage potential women candidates. She cites the myth that women don't win as often as men. Of course, more men are in politics, but when women do run they often win mayoralties or state senate seats. And with more women running, more will undoubtedly be winning.

Another myth Smeal lays to rest is that a woman has to be a lawyer or have better credentials than her male opposition. This is not necessarily so. Although a law degree helps, women politicians have also been nurses, teachers, and housewives. Their experience in organizations or grassroots–level politics is what can qualify them as a candidate.

Finally, Smeal tackles the myth that women can't take losing. Actually, she says, women politicians are more likely to go the distance. At the time she was writing, 76 percent of female state legislators intended to seek other offices in the future compared to 62 percent of their male counterparts. Women who are competitive, bright, and savvy *expect* to win and take a loss only as a lesson in how to do better the next time.

Jeane Kirkpatrick, former U.S. Ambassador to the United Nations, considers the question of why women underestimate themselves as to running for office. She notes that many women don't believe they have leadership qualities. This is especially true of women who have been brought up to be submissive, loving, and gentle. And yet, she points out, there is no biological reason why women cannot be as tough and as assertive as men.

Mrs. Kirkpatrick's book, *Political Woman*, was written over a decade ago, but girls are still brought up differently from boys. She quotes another forceful author's way of defining men and women: "What are big boys made of? What are big boys made of? Independence, aggression, courage, unsentimentality..." et cetera. "What are big girls made of? What are big girls made of? Passivity, fragility, noncompetitiveness..." and other wimpy qualities.

Parents still bring girls up to be the weaker sex, but as women conquer the fields of medicine, law, *and* politics, they will bring up their daughters to think in more positive ways. Then men, Mrs. Kirkpatrick says, will have a harder time hampering women "...in their efforts to participate in power." And indeed, men do obstruct women in politics and will continue to do so until women prove they deserve attention and support in the political world.

With myths behind us, let's consider reality—the reality of running for office, whether for a seat on the local school board or in the United States Senate. Let's consider the thinking behind a woman's decision to become a candidate.

This is a *decision to run*, not a declaration of candidacy; that comes later. It's the same kind of decision process you go through when you are considering a high school, college, or graduate school. You weigh the pros and cons and then make up your mind.

Actually, being a female in an electoral race can be an advantage, says Eleanor Smeal. She found in a survey that women will vote for women candidates. Women make up a large portion of the electorate and can give women the needed political clout. Women want other women in office, Smeal says, because "... electing more women will advance the status of women in politics and would help society." Also, her survey showed that women believed female candidates often had better qualifications for office, and that they were at least as well qualified as men.

Many women candidates themselves came around to this way of thinking. One legislator initially thought she was underqualified. Later she realized, "The other people who were going to run were not even as well qualified as I was!" Besides, she said, "I want to be in on making the rules. I'm tired of others doing it."

Another encouraging point for women: They need not necessarily be major officeholders to seek higher public office. Their "better qualifications" can include being a housewife—but a housewife who is community-minded. Housewives, or single people, can take one of two routes to local, state, or national office: They can be enthusiastic volunteers who make themselves known in the community, or they can work within the structure of a political party.

That is not to say that students who seek political careers should not major in government or social sciences or even aim for law school. It is merely to point out that many women get into the field while the laundry's running and the kids are in school.

Jeane Kirkpatrick quotes some state legislators who used volunteer work as a stepping-stone to office. One assemblywoman commented, "After years of working with the Urban League and civil rights groups, I just knew something had to be done about the problems I encountered." For this woman, that "something" was running for office.

Volunteering develops all kinds of skills. Women learn how to run meetings, set an agenda, solve problems. They develop an interest in local issues and learn to work with people.

These skills comprise leadership qualities—the very qualities needed to be successful in office. For instance, experience in mobilizing forces for a new library can help when it comes to lining up supporters for a floor vote.

Barbara Trafton, a Maine state legislator and Democratic National Committeewoman, is the author of *Women Winning: How to Run for Office*. In it she lists ten questions political candidates should ask themselves when considering a run. Her first question: "Are you physically, emotionally, and mentally prepared...for the campaign trail?" Stated differently, does a woman have the energy and stubbornness of a mule, the nerves of a skydiver, and a mind like a steel trap? If the answer is yes, she'll make the run!

Physical fitness, says Trafton, includes running up and down stairs for her constituents. Lots of potential voters live six flights up! You also have to campaign longer than a man might, because it may take people longer to recognize you as a serious candidate. Women need to work harder to achieve the same goals that men seek.

Women who feel strain and stress would be wise not to run for office. Politics can be a tough field, and accusations and innuendos can bring hurt. Follow any race and you'll see how much mud some candidates will sling to defeat an opponent. A woman must be sure that she can take this treatment for a whole campaign. Also, she must accept the possibility of losing.

Finally, having a mental "quick draw" is a must. Although a woman doesn't need to recite the state charter or the city by-laws, she must be quick and accurate with facts, names, figures, and issues.

Kirkpatrick believes that women must be self-confident to run. Not all women are sure of themselves at the beginning. She divides those considering a run into two groups: the office seekers and the ready recruits. The former do not hesitate to run; the latter are eager but timid.

The bottom line here is that even strong-minded women waver. Self-messages such as "I may not win" or "I may not get the help I need" are common. One state legislator cited in Kirkpatrick's book declared: "I said to my husband that I would like to run. I couldn't believe it was *my* voice saying that!"

Emotional fitness can be summed up in the words of another of Kirkpatrick's interviewees: "Until we change our own attitudes about us, they [men] won't change their attitudes about us. When I'm passed over for something I deserve, I'm going to say, 'That's ...[no way] to treat me after everything I've done for the party.'"

Another question was raised by Barbara Trafton about considering office: "Does a woman candidate have a background, whether political or volunteer-directed, that would make people want to vote for her?" Does her record show that she is concerned about her community and can represent its interests?

Women take different routes to show their concern. One city councilwoman reached her goal through community activity. When challenged by a male opponent on whether she could deal effectively with road problems and public service, she countered with: "I go over the same potholes as you and I have the same trash problems you do!"

Timing plays an important part in seeking office. Barbara Trafton poses this question: "Have you decided that this is the right year to run?"

Eleanor Smeal concurs on timing. She says that a political seat must be "winnable." There is no point going after an incumbent (a person already holding the office) who obviously will win the next race. This is especially true of a member of the majority party. An ideal race in which to run is an "open" race. If a public-minded woman has a solid political or volunteer background and support from an energetic group of people, there is no reason why she cannot win an open seat.

That is rarely the case, however; usually she must decide to challenge an incumbent. If that is her decision, she must be sure she has an ample war chest. It takes a lot of money to defeat an incumbent.

A candidate must find out several things about the person she is challenging did he or she win election? By what majority. What are the person's electoral weaknesses? Strengths? Record in office? Knowing these facts will help her decide on her campaign strategy.

A fact favoring a run against an incumbent is that he or (yes!) she may not have made a good record. Also, voters are turned off by legislators or local officeholders who do not seem sensitive to community needs. Many women, then, run as "reform" candidates. They get into office because people want change. Since women characteristically want changes in the political system, running against the tide is not unappealing to them. They often support activist issues such as control of domestic violence, maternity leave, and child abuse. Many women, however, run on "traditional" platforms, rounding them out with women's issues.

A woman, then, needs to consider the timing of her run. As we've found out, she may win that race: (1) if she appears well qualified; (2) if issues in her community or district propel her into politics; and (3) if she has the backbone to face conflict.

The last point—facing conflict—should not be overlooked, especially if a woman wins and finds herself face-to-face with the trade-offs that are part of practical politics. In a democracy, politicians deal in a currency known as "obligations," defined as "...indebtedness, as for favor." It is a high-level game of "you-scratch-my-back-and-I'll-scratch-yours."

Because so many decisions and tasks are expected of our elected officials, it is nearly impossible for them to study each piece of legislation in detail before passing judgment on it. Sometimes they are likely to vote for or against a measure to create or pay off an obligation.

As another example, a popular political leader may help to raise funds or generate votes for a colleague. This creates an obligation that the leader may use when he or she needs support on an issue.

There can be a fine line between a legitimate political obligation and one that is either questionable or dishonest. A politician may find herself obligated to support legislation that she not only opposes but suspects is unethical. For example, she may be asked to vote for tax relief for an individual or an industry she does not feel deserves it, or to support a government contract for a company whose bid does not qualify for the award. To a person of high moral and ethical standards, these could be situations that she will not accept. In such a case she might look for another career rather than face the prospect of dealing in political "sleaze."

Having been elected to office, she might decide not to run for reelection—or just the reverse: to run hard to stay in office in order to give politics a better image by her independent example.

Chapter **VIII**

Running for Office

She has decided. She'll run. And that decision to become an elected official will ultimately involve many other people. The new candidate needs support from a phalanx of friends, volunteers, business associates, and political allies.

"A campaign requires asking others for support," Jeane Kirkpatrick explains. Some support may be quickly forthcoming—the remainder requires a skillful "hard sell." A female (or male) candidate must have the ability "to build an organization and attract helpers," Mrs. Kirkpatrick continues; the candidate has to sell herself in the political sense, taking advantage of opportunities to promote her candidacy.

For the most part, supporters will be volunteers. These unpaid, loyal workers will work hard because they consider the candidate worth their time and effort. Belief in her work comes naturally to the true politician. Her enthusiasm will ignite her supporters' enthusiasm.

The candidate's volunteer army will do everything from turning out mailings to reminding potential supporters to vote on election day. Because women have always been the "volunteer army," as Eleanor Smeal points out, it may be easier for women candidates to find people to work on a campaign than it is for their male counterparts.

Long before a candidate lines up her supporters, she must develop a strategy for her campaign. Barbara Trafton points out that women need a "game plan" that is realistic and tough-minded. Women need to be "...more competitive, spend more [money], and be more demanding." Translated, that means they must run like male candidates. These hard-boiled qualities have always been part of a man's political toolkit. Women are still struggling to make toughness a part of their campaign strategy.

Barbara Trafton holds that a candidate can develop an effective strategy if she sends a strong message to her constituents, knows the issues, and learns the voters' moods. A candidate's message must clarify why she is running for office. Once she articulates the motivation behind her run—a desire to make changes in her district, or an overriding interest in women's issues—she will have her strategy down cold.

The conscientious candidate will then see that her message gets to the media, decorates bumper stickers, adorns T-shirts—in short, becomes so well known that she is instantly identifiable.

Knowing the issues is as important for a candidate as developing her strategy. She need not be an expert in every area, but she must be familiar with the issues of interest to her voters. And she must *listen* to her voters. Her constituents' major concerns may be for road improvements or the reopening of a factory. A candidate who focuses on local problems will usually gain strong backing.

The woman running for office must be savvy on issues that are traditionally men's as well as women's. She must be able to talk about public works and business regulations as easily as she discusses day care and maternity leave. But experts emphasize that women *must* run as women. Ruth Mandel, Director of the Center for the American Woman and Politics at Rutgers University, says that one must be able to say, "I am a woman and I represent *all* my voters, men and women." One of Jeane Kirkpatrick's women-in-office commented: "You cannot be a woman who is trying to be a man. You've got to be yourself...and be proud of being a woman."

Women may work for women's issues, but no two female campaigns will be alike. Every district, city, or state has its own customs, its pet issues. A woman from Maine will have different matters on her mind than will a woman from New York. Women can be helpful to other women, but they are not political clones.

The candidate soon finds that the potential voter is a moving target. The voters may change their minds many times during a campaign—and even on Election Day! Voters may be loyal and sympathetic, or suspicious and undecided. In fact, some voters within one's district or state are not worth spending time and money to attract: staunch members of the opposing party or persons who have not bothered to vote in recent elections. Time and campaign money are better spent on the more promising voters.

These "promising" voters most likely will vote for the woman candidate, but even they must be catered to. What voters want in one section of town, they may not want in another. Thus, the candidate's message must be general *and* specific. She must convince voters that she has their overall interests at heart while still pressing for improvement in specific trouble areas.

Raising funds to support a campaign is another part of the overall strategy. As mentioned before, raising enough money to fund a major campaign is probably the most difficult obstacle a woman candidate faces. (Local political races may not be so financially draining.)

Campaign chest needs range from thousands of dollars for a mayoralty race to over $5.3 million for a U.S. Senate run. The latter figure was raised for a woman Senator, Paula Hawkins of Florida, on her second run for the seat in the early 1980s. The figure would be much higher today.

Whatever the cost of a race, the methods of publicity are similar. Television and other media attention, office operations, printing, and the costs of stumping (traveling and getting out the vote) are all part of the picture. Today especially, exposure is paramount. In this television age, we virtually elect our candidates by personality and power to persuade.

Both men and women need money to fund their campaigns. Men fill their coffers far more easily than their female counterparts. Nowhere is the "old-boy network" more visible than in fund-raising. Men support men because they're a proven political commodity. Only when a woman is outstanding will the men of her party line up behind her.

Fortunately, women are doing better in the political arena. As they become more electable, more men will be willing to put money into their campaigns.

Women are also raising more money because of other women. Powerful women's groups are giving female candidates financial support and pushing them over the top. Helping to do this are fund-raising groups called political action committees (PACs).

The PACs range from endangered-species lobbyists to the National Women's Political Caucus. Nearly all so-called special-interest groups have PAC funds to back candidates—men and women—who are sympathetic to their causes.

Women have several PACs to fall back on. The American Association of University Women and the forthright NOW (National Association for Women) are among those offering financial support. "For the first time, we're seeing financial godmothers," says a spokeswoman for women's causes. Many of these PACs will fund only women who actively support women's issues.

Even when the money is there, women often do not know how to go after it. One major reason why women can't raise as much money as men is that they are more hesitant to ask for it. As women, we have been raised to be subtle about asking for things.

But the time for holding back is past. We must march boldly up to people and organizations to fund what we believe in, *us*. As Kathleen Curry, a spokeswoman for a powerful women's organization, says: "Women have stopped being shrinking violets. I always tell women that if they can't ask for money, they should just go home."

Still, money at the highest levels of political office is hard to come by. Candidates of the lower levels of politics don't need as much money. Alice Travis, who was a candidate for Los Angeles City Controller, says: "When the stakes are low, women can win." She points out that there are more women in the New Hampshire legislature than that of any other state in the country, and the electioneering expenses for these positions were fairly low.

Of course, women cannot be content to win only local and state posts. They must believe they are worthy of the highest positions and go into the political ring swinging.

When a woman candidate has sufficient funds, she begins to use the media to present her ideas. How does she go about projecting these ideas? Eleanor Smeal has some basic questions a candidate should ask herself. The answers to these questions will make her publicity effective. Two of them are: "What professional qualities do you want highlighted?" and "What will you do if elected?"

A campaign "kit" of press clippings, a biography, and issues of the campaign will provide the answers to these basic questions.

Smeal also suggests that a candidate learn all reporters' moves. She will be seeing these faces over and over. Their evaluation of her is crucial to her campaign. And, if she is lively enough to be endorsed in an editorial, she will have hit the media jackpot.

Women going into state and national contests employ all sorts of media techniques. Television, computer phone banks, and even satellites are now available. Mobile satellite trucks make it possible for a person's message to "go live" anywhere. The high-tech age has indeed changed the way candidates campaign. For those after the highest political prizes, door-to-door campaigning is usually a thing of the past—unless the TV cameras tag along.

Technology helps greater numbers of people get to know almost every candidate running for office today. The all-seeing eye of TV can also reflect a candidate's attitudes. For women, that poses a problem that male candidates do not have to consider. Women must decide whether they want to appear "cool" or combative as they campaign. Men don't need to worry about this because their varying styles are accepted.

Many women candidates will not indulge in mud-slinging. It's not their nature. Jeanne Kirkpatrick quotes one state legislator: "I have never spoken against an opponent in any but the most gracious and charming way. I just emphasize my qualifications for the job."

Others are not so reticent. As Mrs. Kirkpatrick effectively puts it: "Some political types need conflict the way fire needs air." Yes, women can conduct fiery races, if that's their style.

In general, however, Mrs. Kirkpatrick found that most of the women legislators she interviewed neither sought conflict nor were bothered by it. Perhaps this balanced attitude contributed to their victories in state government.

But to do well on the campaign trail, Mrs. Kirkpatrick finds that the key ingredient is to enjoy oneself. That's not true only of politics; all career choices should be enjoyable ones. But there is a particular magic to politicking. The candidate is "on stage," adrenalin up, doing what she likes best—communicating with people.

To some politicians campaigning seems to be even more pleasurable than serving in office. One of Kirkpatrick's state legislators said: "Coming into a group where I knew no one...and talking to people and meeting people...I love this...I enjoyed it. I found it exhilarating, not tiring." This is a politician who is likely to win over and over again.

Chapter **IX**

Local Government

"Begin at the beginning," said Alice—and this phrase from *Alice in Wonderland* is surely appropriate to a career in the wonderland of American politics. Rare indeed is the politician who is able to begin anywhere else. Even those who come from political families do not automatically leap into high office. They, too, have to announce that they are running for a political post, win their party's primary, then stand for the general election. Their family name may gain them recognition, but it's no guarantee they'll be elected.

The "beginning" in your case may be a post as seemingly low-profile as a seat on your local school board or town council, or being a committeeperson or township commissioner. But make no mistake—these jobs are anything but insignificant. The former Speaker of the House of Representatives, Thomas ("Tip") O'Neill, has said, "All politics is local." He meant that the trials and tribulations are the same in any political office. The need for excellence is just as important at the grassroots level as it is higher up the ladder.

When you deal with "gut" issues, as you would as a committeeperson or a member of your school board or town council, you can expect fireworks aplenty. You have to be prepared to deal directly with the issues raised by parents, neighbors, and town residents and do your best to respond to their wishes. You really do serve the public in a very personal and direct way.

Even for the most basic local election, you have to attract attention and get the word out about yourself. In politics, modesty will get you nowhere! To be known, you must be seen and heard. You have to put your background, opinions, qualifications, and

Mary Ann Gabel, at right, Republican Committeewoman for Montgomery County, Pennsylvania, hands out literature on Election Day.

accomplishments on paper with an inexpensive handbill or newsletter. You need plenty of printing, volunteer help, campaign time, free publicity, energy, and enthusiasm—and all the money you can get.

You may not need political experience, but in order to run you need to have a political viewpoint. Let's say you're married, have some business administration in your background, and have a young child entering the school system. You may feel that more money should be allocated for school trips and less for sports. If you feel strongly enough about that issue, and if you can get support for your view from other parents, you may have enough backing to run for a school board seat. You may even be forced to run because—although lots of others may be interested—nobody else is willing to tackle the issues you raise. Whether it's by choice or by default, you're running.

Being elected or reelected or moving on to higher office calls for building on your strengths, and that means making sure your constituents know about them. You must list your accomplishments, express your views, and maintain your positions—especially if you have run for office and those views won for you in the first place. If you change your views, which you may do as you gain experience, you must be sure your constituents understand the changes and accept your reasons for making them. All that means a constant effort to get information across with newspaper coverage of your appearances. Even if you're a school board member attending a parent-teachers association meeting, you can benefit from publicity. With a reporter at the meeting, you have a chance to make news of your views.

Karen Bojar, a committeeperson in a Philadelphia neighborhood, expressed her views on reelection in a newspaper article: "I am seeking a second term as a committeeperson to ensure that my neighbors receive the best service and information about the political choices they face. I also want to raise issues affecting women and children in the political arena and work to elect candidates who share these concerns."

Belonging to organizations devoted to political issues is a very important part of running for office. Any woman who holds a city office, for instance, is eligible for membership in Women in Municipal Government (WIMG), a combination forum and support group for women in all phases of city government nationwide. Regional and national meetings are held at which members exchange ideas and information and encourage each others' political efforts. These efforts include working in other governmental organizations, such as the National League of Cities, and statewide governmental activity groups.

At one WIMG meeting held in conjunction with a National League of Cities event, former Texas State Representative Wilhelmina Delco addressed the attendees at a luncheon. She told the members that, to be successful in public life, women need "...the three I's: information, involvement, and investment."

She went on to say, "We need to have the courage to say to our sisters, 'How can you afford not to be what you can be?' You owe it to yourselves to be whatever you want to be. It has finally arrived—that time when women don't have to explain, to apologize, to be the exception, in order to get the job done. We have the ability to bring excitement to [fiscal and social] issues.... It is now time for men to stand by us and for us to stand with each other. We are not alone."

Mary Ann Gabel is the Republican Committeeperson for the East District of Whitemarsh Township, Montgomery County, Pennsylvania. She is one of twenty elected Committee members in the Township; thus, she knows her own corner of this largely Republican area exceptionally well. This is her job, one for which she must stand in the primary election every two years.

A good Republican (or Democratic) Committee member is a joiner. He or she belongs to a variety of organizations and gets to know as many people in the community as possible, to know the "criticisms, enthusiasms, and feelings" of constituents, and tries to help with community problems.

That broad definition only touches the surface of what Mrs. Gabel does in the course of a year. In Pennsylvania every year is an election year, although some are more important than others. To Mrs. Gabel and everyone in the local party—elected, appointed, and volunteer—preparing for an election is a continuous job. It includes selecting leaders, arranging the campaign calendar, and fund-raising. They also distribute campaign literature and work for voter registration, one of the most important items on the long checklist.

Registration involves the use of "street lists," maps of each street in each Committee member's area. It is Mrs. Gabel's job to make sure that every family whose political preference is not known is contacted and asked to register—preferably as Republicans! Last but not least, a letter is distributed to all of Mrs. Gabel's constituents a few days before the election, describing the candidates and the issues.

Things really get busy on the big day. The Committeemembers arrive early to help open the polls and to make sure that party poll workers are there. All day, Mrs. Gabel is busy answering voters' questions (although never telling them how to vote; that is illegal).

Dorothy Smith, Inspector of Elections, registers a voter.

In the late afternoon, she and her coworkers get out their ever-ready street lists and telephone those who have not yet appeared, to remind them to vote. When the polls close she joins the other Committeemembers and polling officials from both parties in tabulating the votes, posting the results at each district, and forwarding these unofficial results to campaign headquarters at the county seat.

The fact that Mary Ann Gabel is in local rather than national politics doesn't bother this dynamic woman in the slightest. Local government is her bailiwick. She knows how important her job is—not just at election time, but throughout the year. "When there's an important local issue," Mrs. Gabel comments, it's the Committee member's job to get people involved—"to get them out to zoning hearings, township supervisors' meetings, or wherever that issue will be talked about. My voters deserve to be told about situations that affect them. When they attend meetings with a united front, they can make a difference."

Another big job, she says, is looking for qualified people to run for office. If they're women, all the better, but Mrs. Gabel is more interested in qualifications and interest. "People lack interest because local politics is time-consuming," she says. "So, during the year we are always looking for people to run for township supervisor, school board members, and other positions. Months before the primaries, we're out there asking the incumbents if they want to run again, and if not, finding potential replacements."

Mary Ann Gabel and her associates work beyond the township level to help determine the slate for their county. Offices such as county commissioner, district attorney, register of wills, treasurer, and state representatives and senators are among the many where the party involves all its members and determines who will run.

Mary Ann Gabel is not from a political family, but she found that as a Home Economics major at Penn State University she nearly always gave a political theme to the parties and receptions she designed as part of her curriculum. Her minor, Early Childhood Development, came into the picture when as a young bride she got involved in her first political campaign. "Politics is a form of teaching," she says today, "and I was teaching school at the time. Once I became involved, I stayed involved."

Her first post beyond that of vounteer was as local polling machine inspector, in 1972. "I've been at it ever since."

With activities such as Penn State Alumni Association, boating, reading, theater, and the care of two homes, why does this high-energy woman continue her political activity? "Because I see being a Committeewoman as a way to give something back to this community. I'd like to think I'm doing something to make it an area to be proud of."

What better political motivation could there be?

One of the most visible posts for women is that of mayor. Some 15 percent of this country's mayors are women. Many of them are mayors of small towns or boroughs; others head some of the largest cities in the nation. In Texas, for example, Her Honor the Mayor presides in the four major cities—Houston, Dallas, Galveston, and Corpus Christi.

Black women are beginning to make a dent in the mayoral picture, too. One woman who is very visible is Carrie Saxon Perry, Mayor of Hartford, the capital of Connecticut. Mrs. Perry is the prototype political woman, a no-nonsense, outspoken, farsighted politician. She has great plans for Hartford and means to see them through, but that may not be so easy. The mayoralty in Hartford pays under $20,000 and is regarded as largely ceremonial (Hartford, like several other cities, has a "weak mayor" form of city administration). But Mrs. Perry hopes to change that. She has veto power over the budget drawn up by the City Council and the City Manager.

Perry wants to reduce the city's poverty problem. Her hopes for Hartford's future are being translated into task force programs and study groups. As an action-oriented mayor she encourages community meetings, educational programs, and corporation involvement (Hartford is a hub of the insurance industry). She wants to turn this historical community into a financially healthy, equal-opportunity city.

Mayors differ in their power and their pay. Katherine Whitmere, Mayor of Houston, receives $105,000 a year. She is also the city's boss; unlike Mrs. Perry, she has no city manager to defer to.

Power varies with the other women mayors in Texas. It depends upon the city charter and other factors. Galveston, Corpus Christi, Houston, and Dallas (and other cities in Texas. Oklahoma, and Louisiana) are still reeling from the oil bust of the mid-eighties. The women mayors have tried to emphasize other industries such as tourism and aerospace to offset the decline in petroleum.

Texas is proud of its unusual number of women mayors, but these heads of municipal government have a narrow line to walk with their constituents. Texas women—and Southern women in general—must appear gentle, genteel, and modest, politically powerful or not. The four mayors are all of that—but there's steel under their quiet rule. Annette Strause, Mayor of Dallas, admits, "Southern women are coddled...but we are also smart. We know how to smile and get things done, too."

Barbara Jordan, a former member of the United States Congress and now a Professor of Government Policy at the University of Texas, says, "If you are a politician and you are female and you are Texan...you must exude confidence, but you must always, and I underscore always, be a lady. Texans do not want you to be one of the boys."

These Texas women must depend somewhat on male support to remain in office, and that support is often half-hearted. But one city leader, Mayor Jean Grace of Carmel, California, got into office with the wholehearted support of a male. Clint Eastwood, movie star and mayor of Carmel in the late 1980s, campaigned for Ms. Grace to succeed him.

But most mayors or others in elective office do not have Ms. Grace's unique situation. They may, like Juanita Crabb, Mayor of Binghamton, New York, head fairly large cities that face problems unheard-of in picturesque Carmel. Mrs.Crabb addresses her city's concerns aided by a predominantly male but sympathetic City Council. She is also well liked by the city's largely male police and fire departments.

A mayor's job is a grab bag in many ways. In Mayor Crabb's case the grab bag includes everything from encouraging new businesses to planning the budget. At times her duties become even more diversified. Recently three tank cars containing butane gas overturned at the railroad station. Mayor Crabb spent thirteen hours helping to move residents to the high school gymnasium and seeing that they had food. This kind of contribution is typical of dedicated officials. They care about the people who cared enough to vote for them.

Political success is often a case of being in the right place at the right time. That is how Dianne Feinstein, former Mayor of San Francisco, became nationally known almost from the day she took office. Being lucky or, as in Feinstein's case, being thrust in the spotlight because of others' misfortunes may get a politician into office, but it takes real talent to stay there.

Feinstein had run twice for mayor unsuccessfully. Her later bid for a seat on the Board of Supervisors was successful. In fact, because she received more votes than any other candidate, she automatically became Board President. In was from that post that Feinstein was appointed Mayor by her fellow Board members after the assassination of Mayor George Moscone and Supervisor Harvey Milk by another member of the Board.

Dianne Feinstein had to face the awesome responsibilities of government while coping with a devastating personal crisis. Shortly before the events that propelled Feinstein into office, her husband had died of cancer. And her trip to the Himalayas in an effort to regain her perspective had ended in serious illness. She had just about decided to complete her term as Supervisor and leave public life.

But, as she has said, "There's a saying in politics, 'Winning isn't everything, but defeat has absolutely nothing to recommend it.'" So Dianne Feinstein, with her reputation as a tough but even-handed administrator, accepted the leadership role.

Her first task was to get a demoralized city administration functioning again. That meant carrying on the political mandate of Mayor Moscone, even though he had defeated her in her most recent run for the office. But after winning handily on her own at the first opportunity, she began to run the city more to her own liking.

It was to the people's liking as well. She bit more than one bullet on taxes, balanced city budgets, added to the police department, and turned her workaholic ways loose on one segment of city government after another—including bringing women into the higher levels of city management.

Not all her political decisions were popular. She vetoed a controversial proposal that would have compensated the live-in companions of city workers and as a result was forced into a recall election. The voters agreed with her position that this and similar legislation would bankrupt the city. She scored an 83 percent victory on the recall vote and went on to win decisively later in the regular election for her second term.

Since the law did not permit her to run for a third term, Feinstein was faced once more with a career decision after more than eight years at the helm. Her choice was a large step up: She would test the waters for a run at the California governorship in 1990. As a northern Californian and a Democrat she has the challenge of becoming better known in southern California, where the power base is. Her political views, although moderate, must work against a strongly conservative bias in the southern part of the state. However, she has the money—over $50,000, and another $2.5 million in pledges—plus the personality and perseverance to mount a solid campaign.

Whether or not the political winds blow her way, Feinstein will campaign in her own way, with little or no help from political consultants. Too many candidates, she believes, allow consultants to run their campaigns. It's too easy, she says, for candidates to blame their consultants for their own shortcomings. Speaking to the authors of *Momentum: Women in American Politics Now*, she said: "I've...got to say I never have [given my campaign over to a consultant]. I've won and I've lost, and I've never blamed a consultant for my loss. I think when you have weak candidates, they give themselves over to a political consultant and say, 'Here, merchandise me'...a big mistake, because the chances are that that political candidate isn't going to know what to do when they get elected."

That is one problem Dianne Feinstein isn't likely to have! After more than eighteen years in big-city politics, she believes she has what's needed to govern America's second-largest state.

Chapter **X**

State Politics

Two political changes are occurring at once. Both affect the future of women in politics.

First, the focus of political action is moving from the national to the state level. During the Reagan administration much of the federal government's role was transferred to the states, especially in the area of social programs. Appropriately, many women candidates at the state level have won election by supporting social action. Once in office, they have been pleased to find, as Marilyn Gardner wrote in *The Christian Science Monitor*, that "...the legislative process moves more quickly [at the state level] and accomplishments are more visible."

Nancy Kassebaum, Republican Senator from Kansas, expressed the change well when she said, "Washington has become almost moribund in the process of trying to accomplish anything. The vitality and ingenuity lie in state government, and women are leading the way."

That indeed appears to be the case, for the second trend is a great increase in the number of women state legislators. It is accompanied by an equal increase in enthusiasm about the future of women in state-level politics.

This was made quite clear during the 1987 convention of the Forum of State Legislators, sponsored by the Center for the American Woman and Politics.

The Forum noted that there were 1,168 women state legislators, or 16 percent of the total. Four years earlier those numbers were 991 and 13 percent. But with women making up nearly 55 percent of the American population, more states need to follow the lead of

Ruth B. Harper, member of the Pennsylvania House of Representatives, meets with children of the Sunshine Foundation Day Care Center in Philadelphia. Mrs. Harper purchased the house for working mothers in 1988.

Maine, where three out of every ten legislators are women. Somewhat different percentages accent the greater opportunity for women at the state rather than the federal level: There are just two women Senators and twenty-five Representatives—only 5 percent of the total.

However, those few women and their predecessors in Congress have a degree of power. At the Forum, Federal Trade Commission member Patricia P. Bailey said, "Most of the federal legislation that has had a positive impact on women has been introduced by women or enacted because they persuaded men to join them." (A perfect example is the effort put forth by former Congresswoman Shirley Chisholm of New York to have domestic workers covered by minimum wage legislation.)

Although women can and do make a difference, the changes that women state legislators can make in the political process are viewed differently—even by women state legislators. In telling Forum participants that women can bring a different perspective to politics and to public policy, Illinois State Senator Joyce Holmberg said, "I predict we'll have a very different United States of America when more legislators are female."

The view that women will not materially change the ways of state politics was expressed at the Forum by State Representative Gracia Backer of Missouri: "I work on issues because I believe in them and because they're important to my district and my state. I'm tired of women being treated as a novelty act."

Does that mean that, if they are to exert power at the state level, women must be a part of the "old boy network"? Forum participants disagreed. Jean Marie Brough, Republican floor leader in the Washington State House of Representatives, said: "I don't like the process, but in order to make a change, you have to get power, and in order to get power you have to play the system." Speaking of the informal drinks-and-poker get-togethers at which many political decisions are made, Brough said, "I simply join [the men], but I try not to drink. And I won't play basketball with them on Wednesday nights. I fear for life and limb!" In concluding, Brough discussed the "old girl" network she and other women had begun, to which "old boys" were not invited. "One time we met in the women's lounge," she said. "That was really fun."

Vera Katz, speaker of the Oregon House of Representatives,

does not quite hold that view. She says that women should try to attend informal sessions with men because, "It's an environment that can be used to discuss issues or discuss you behind your back. Indeed, it is better to be there!" She does not believe, however, that women should play the same games the same way. "[Once you have reached a leadership position], you have a responsibility to do it differently," she said.

Reaching a leadership position in state government started early—at age twenty-three—for Mary Landrieu when she campaigned for the Louisiana State Assembly and won. Now, with a few years' experience behind her, Landrieu, the oldest child of former Mayor Moon Landrieu of New Orleans, has won election as State Treasurer.

The person least surprised by Landrieu's victory was Donna Brasile, her campaign manager. Brasile, who is black, characterized Landrieu as "one of the boldest white women I've ever seen in my life." Brasile admired the way Landrieu worked the telephones every day, starting at 8:00 A.M. Landrieu made no secret of her ambitions and was anything but shy about the all-important matter of fund-raising. Not the least of Landrieu's smart moves was hiring a savvy campaign manager: Brasile!

Women aspiring to state office are urged to make end runs if a direct assault isn't possible. Celinda Lake, director of candidate services for the Women's Campaign Fund, suggests tactics such as looking for open seats, where no incumbent is running. These are apt to arise when shifts in population bring about reapportionment or reorganization of existing voting districts. In other words, a new piece of "political pie" becomes available. It can happen, too, when male officeholders announce plans to run for other offices. Of course, male legislators, judges, or other elected state officials may be vulnerable on the basis of past performance—another way for women to run, and win.

Women who run for state office (or any office, for that matter) can themselves become vulnerable. The story of Rose Bird is ample proof that the seas of politics are often stormy.

Miss Bird, a gifted attorney and onetime teacher at Stanford University Law School, was appointed Chief Justice of the California Supreme Court in 1977 by then Governor Jerry Brown. (Bird had been the state's Secretary of Agriculture and Services.)

Governor Brown, no stranger to controversy, appointed several women to influential positions in California government. But he may have overreached in naming the young (age forty at the time) and beautiful Rose Bird not as a Supreme Court Justice but as Chief Justice. (Some hold that while the move acknowledged Bird's legal capabilities, it was also made in part to shake up the Establishment.)

In any case, many California attorneys resented the appointment, in part because Bird was a woman, but also because she was young for the position. She had been placed in the top post without even having served as a judge in a lower court.

Governors (and Presidents, for that matter) make Supreme Court appointments that reflect their own political beliefs. In Rose Bird's case, Governor Brown's appointment was a boost for the liberals. But in California, Court Justices, even though initially appointed, must stand periodically for reelection. During her years as Chief Justice, Bird had won twice, but opposition to her grew as the political climate changed from liberal to conservative in the late 1970s.

In 1978 California voters reinstated capital punishment, with which liberals by and large disagree. By 1986, when opposition to Bird had become a well-organized effort, there had still been no executions under the new law. It was alleged by her opponents that Rose Bird's own successful battle against cancer had given her an outlook on life that made it difficult for her to agree with the death penalty. It was also alleged that she had not been cured but actually was dying of cancer.

Conservative politicians and law-and-order advocates were the most vocal and best-organized groups opposing Bird's reelection. As the fight became more vicious, Bird was urged by her supporters to refute the soft-on-crime allegations. During her tenure on the Court the criminal conviction rate had actually increased, and sentences had become longer. Instead, she remained largely above the battle.

She was also urged to accept support from environmentalists, minorities, and organized labor, three groups that would logically benefit from her position on issues affecting them. Again, she refused, believing that if she accepted their help she would be obligated to them and therefore unable to administer justice fairly.

Although not openly so called, the "get Rose Bird" campaign was successful, and she was relieved of her position as Chief Justice. How much did her being a woman have to do with her defeat? Could a male Chief Justice of similar Democratic leanings have survived the conservative-fueled recall campaign that Bird lost? Those questions are hard to answer. The fact that she is a woman, coupled with elements of her personality, may have been factors; her presence is hard to ignore.

For one thing, she has never married, a fact that was viewed negatively by some and used against her. Her forthrightness apparently bothered others. She was perceived by many as a "poker-face" in her role as a no-nonsense Chief Justice. Former Governor Brown took no part in her 1986 campaign. The fact that she made little effort to refute her critics or return the mud that was slung at her probably contributed to her defeat. (It can be argued that a man placed in a similar position would have gone down swinging and slinging; she preferred to go out with style. After her ouster, she said she was taking her defeat "...like a man.")

Since that defeat, Rose Bird has done television commentary for two California stations—again, not without arousing emotions on both sides of her views. She does not plan to practice law, at least not in California. She is writing a book about her years as Chief Justice and her 1986 defeat as she considers her future.

There is no question about the future for two Pennsylvania State Representatives, Ruth B. Harper and Frances Weston. Although they come from districts in Philadelphia with very different needs and are of opposing political parties, these two women have won reelection handily.

Ruth B. Harper is in her seventh two-year term as a member of the Pennsylvania House of Representatives. The legislative district that she represents is all too typical of today's inner city. Mrs. Harper tackles the problems with a combination of optimism, reality, toughness, and visibility—and she gets results.

For instance, when homes in the Logan section of her district began to sink and become unlivable, she sponsored legislation to help those families whose homes were being condemned and whose life savings were threatened. Through her vigorous action, more than $5.3 million in state funds were allocated to the Logan

Assistance Corporation, a public body formed to purchase and rehabilitate replacement homes from the Philadelphia Redevelopment Authority. This is her proudest accomplishment in her legislative career. In second place is her work to fund Philadelphia's Afro-American History Museum and bring it under the supervision of the Pennsylvania Museum and Historical Commission.

Currently Mrs. Harper is sponsoring tougher laws against drug trafficking; working to enact a law creating a training program to qualify people to provide day care in their homes; and sponsoring a bill to assure tenant rights and landlord responsibilities.

"What drives me as a legislator is helping people," she said during an interview. "And to help, you have to be visible, to let people know they can count on you. I'm very interested in education. When I found out that two of our state colleges—Cheyney and Lincoln—were badly in need of repairs, I organized a bus trip to Harrisburg. It got a lot of publicity, and that eventually led to $10 million in appropriations to bring those colleges up to the level of the others in the system. I'm proud of that accomplishment."

Mrs. Harper was a businesswoman before becoming a legislator, and she credits that experience—operating a charm school and modeling agency—with making her legislative career possible. "I was a shy person, but I learned modeling from someone who helped me overcome shyness. And when I did get interested in politics, my own business gave me two things, confidence and name recognition," she said. "About that time, I joined the National Women's Political Caucus. I started supporting candidates I believed in. And then the wife of one of our City Councilmen suggested that somebody run for Committeeman—or Committeeperson—for my neighborhood. The 'somebody' she had in mind was me. I filed, ran, and won.

"Lots of people don't want to be Committee members. They don't think it's important because you're at the bottom of the ladder. But it *is* important, because the Committeeperson works right with the people in the neighborhood. If you do your job well, the ward leader gets to know you can be depended on, and you move up. That's what I did."

Move up she did, once she was elected to the legislature. Although she has always run as an independent Democrat with

68   CAREERS FOR WOMEN IN POLITICS

RICHARD S. LEE PHOTO

Frances Weston, Pennsylvania State Representative from Philadelphia, with her police officer-husband, Edward, and their daughters Kaitlyn (left) and Bridget.

little party support, she has become the Majority Chairman of the Urban Affairs Committee. While seniority assured her a place on this important committee, she earned the chairmanship on her own strengths. She is also a National Democratic Party Committeewoman, a post to which she was elected by party officials statewide. She is in her third four-year term and was a Superdelegate to the 1988 Democratic National Convention.

When asked why more women do not become involved in politics, Mrs. Harper said, "One reason is that men don't give money to women candidates as they would to men. Money-raising is tough. We expect women to raise money for men candidates, but it doesn't work the other way." Also, Mrs. Harper agreed with Dr. Nagel of the University of Pennsylvania that politics is confrontational and many women don't like the conflict. "Men say to me, 'You're a special kind of woman to be in politics,'" she added with a twinkle. "I'm not sure that's a compliment!"

"Once women are in office," she continued, "they're effective —*if* they fight when they're right. I remember a woman legislator who inherited her husband's seat. She was just too quiet to make it, and she didn't last. But politics is risky for women, just as business is. A lot of educated women would rather teach school or do something else that's more a sure thing. That's another reason women don't run."

As for playing the power game, Ruth Harper doesn't work that way. "I'm straight-out," she said. "If I believe in a piece of legislation, I support it, and I let the sponsor know I supported it. Next time, when *I* need support, I'll get it.

"One afternoon, there was some rural legislation on the [House] floor. Since it didn't concern most of the city legislators, they simply left. Just two of us were there from Philadelphia. The other city legislator asked me, 'Why are you still here?' And I said, 'I think I should be here to vote for their bill.' He said, 'Me, too.' We did—and don't think those rural legislators didn't help when some of my urban issues came up for consideration!"

The other Pennsylvania State Representative, Frances Weston, first ran for the legislature at age twenty-five. She is a Republican —not an advantage in a state that is currently under a Democratic administration—and she has two young children. All this makes it difficult for her to manage a political career.

Initially, Representative Weston had served her largely Democratic district as a Republican Committee member. When the party needed a candidate to try to oust a somewhat complacent Democratic incumbent, Mrs. Weston decided to try. She had the support of one of the district's two ward leaders and was able to rally the other with her combination of neighborhood strength and natural political know-how. (A background in political science also led to further interest in the community.)

Also, she says, "It didn't hurt that I was one of ten in the family or that my parents had been politically active all my life. Everyone—my brothers and sisters and my parents—got behind me and worked. We all campaigned hard. One thing that helps around here is that this is a neighborhood of single-family homes, not high-rise apartments. It's easier to get around and meet people. When we scored that upset victory, it was the greatest thrill of my life."

In 1988 she won her fifth two-year term, but the state legislature has not been her only campaign. She was the Republican candidate for City Controller in 1983, a year in which Republican politicians were not favored.

How does it feel to be a woman—and a young, attractive woman at that—in what is still perceived as a man's game? "Some legislators, especially older men from rural sections of the state, have subconscious prejudices. It's nothing specific, but they tend not to take women legislators seriously. I've found in campaigning that some women tend not to see me as a plausible legislator, either!"

When asked about women's issues, Mrs. Weston replied, "I don't especially address women's problems. Yes, I'll support Republican organizations that help women get elected, and I'll help women of my party who are running—but legislatively I'm a big believer in service back home.

"Three Republican women are running for the General Assembly this fall [1988], and there ought to be more. But money is the tough part. I do think that as more women get into business, the professions, and appointive politics, they'll form their own money-raising network for women candidates. It won't be tomorrow, though."

When asked how she manages a career, a family, and commuting five hours to and from the state capital three times a week, Frances Weston said, "My husband is the reason. Ed has taken an active role in my career from day one. I just couldn't do it if he didn't participate."

Is her career more demanding than those of other women working outside the home? "My schedule with the kids has to be, on balance, worse than most women with children and careers. Ed is a police officer with six days on and two off, then his shift changes—sometimes he works nights, sometimes days. I have a great woman in the neighborhood who takes the girls during the day, and somehow we work it out. But I'm not at home many evenings and some weekends. I worry about not always being with the kids in their formative years, but the time Ed and I do spend with them is real 'quality time'—and I hope my girls, when they get older, will understand more about life because they have a mother like me. Our house is full of good times, and that may be partly because I have an exciting life of my own. I bring that enthusiasm back home and we are all so happy to see each other."

Chapter **XI**

The Rare Nine: Women Governors

"Rare" is indeed the word when you consider that there are fifty states in the nation and that each state usually elects a governor every four years. If we take only the last 75 years (when most of the present states were part of the Union), there would have been approximately eighteen governors per state. Multiply eighteen times the fifty states and you have more than 900 governors. But only nine have been women!

The first two, Nellie Tayloe Ross of Wyoming and Miriam ("Ma") Ferguson of Texas, were elected in 1925. Governor Ferguson served until 1927 and again from 1933 through 1935. More than thirty years were to pass before another woman governed a state.

The third candidate, Lurleen Wallace, was elected Governor of Alabama in 1967 because her husband, Governor George Wallace, could not succeed himself in office according to state law. Not until the late Ella Grasso became Governor of Connecticut in 1975 and Dixy Lee Ray took over the reins in Washington State two years later were women governors taken at all seriously.

As of 1988, Martha Layne Collins was completing her term as Governor of Kentucky, Kay Orr was the first woman Governor of Nebraska, Madeleine Kunin was in her third two-year term as Governor of Vermont, and "Auntie Rose" Mofford had just become Arizona's first woman Governor.

The last three make interesting stories.

In 1986 Kay Orr became the nation's first elected Republican woman governor. She set another precedent in her campaign by running against another woman, Helen Boosalis, the Democratic former Mayor of Lincoln.

Madeleine Kunin, Governor of Vermont, the seventh woman governor in the United States.

The all-woman race developed when the democratic Governor, Robert Kerrey, announced that he would not run for reelection. Boosalis had made history herself by becoming the first woman mayor of a city of 100,000 or more. She came to the office after sixteen years' service in the City Council. She had been a high-energy legislator, having served as the first woman president of the U.S. Conference of Mayors in 1981 and 1982. Following this, she became Director of the Nebraska Department on Aging in 1983—a scrappy, formidable contender.

Orr, no mean campaigner herself, came to the race after twenty-two years of Republican political activity. She began as a precinct captain in 1964 and later served as chief of staff to then Governor Charles Thone. He appointed her State Treasurer, and she won election to her own four-year term in 1982. Kay Orr distinguished herself in office by saving the state $1 million through changing state investments to interest-bearing accounts. Known for her quiet efficiency and direct, personal campaign style, she rode to victory on the crest of Ronald Reagan's popularity in the predominantly Republican state.

Money—and talk of money—played a large part in the campaign. Kay Orr campaigned on the success of the Reagan administration's policies, pointing as well to the money she had saved the state. Her campaign was supported as well by major fund-raising among Nebraska Republicans.

The issue around which the campaign was fought turned out to be school consolidation. Helen Boosalis campaigned for merging rural and urban schools to improve overall education. Kay Orr campaigned—successfully—*not* to consolidate. She argued that merging the schools would call for a one-cent increase in the state sales tax. As an amusing aftermath to her election victory, Governor Orr was chosen "Man of the Year" by the Omaha Club. Her response on accepting the honor: "I'm pleased you consider me woman enough to be your man of the year!"

Madeleine Kunin, the third Democratic governor of Vermont since the Civil War and the seventh woman governor in the United States, reached that position thanks to the support of her physician husband, her family of four children, and through her own hard work.

To make her story even more untypical, she is an immigrant, brought to this country by her mother in 1940 to escape from Hitler's Germany. Although she grew up as a typical American, the child Madeleine May nevertheless remembered her early experiences. These directly influenced her eventual entry into politics. In an interview with *Working Woman* magazine, Kunin explained it this way: "Quite unconsciously, I absorbed the knowledge that instead of being an uninvolved observer and potential victim, I could be in a position of active influence and control."

Doing so would take quite a few years.

Her first career was as a journalist. She worked as a waitress to help pay her way through the University of Massachusetts. She majored in history, graduated with honors, and earned a master's degree from the Columbia University Graduate School of Journalism. From there, she took a job with the Burlington [Vermont] *Free Press*. Soon after, she married Arthur Kunin, worked as a TV writer-producer, and spent the next several years raising her children.

Her first political venture was a no-win. In 1972 she was nominated for a Democratic Caucus, lost by a few votes—but ran successfully for the state House of Representatives, where she served until 1978. Then she decided to run for lieutenant governor (a separate elective office in Vermont). She won two two-year terms, the second with nearly 60 percent of the vote even in the face of strong Republican popularity.

Kunin was not able to pick up enough votes to win her first race for governor, but in her second run for lieutenant governor she was extraordinarily successful at fund-raising. She credits this fact with having given her the credibility to run for governor, lose the election, yet come back to win. Because that's exactly what happened in 1984.

Much of her funding came from groups in the women's movement, and her slim victory (50.02 percent of the vote) was due to support from the women's movement. Fifty-three percent of women voted for her, 35 percent for her male opponent.

In office, her encouraging, productive style has delivered results for the state and popularity for her. A 76 percent approval rating demonstrates that popularity. Her abilities have resulted in the passage of many pieces of legislation she favored, including eight environmental protection and improvement laws.

Madeleine Kunin believes that the greatest obstacle women face in running for office is their own passive tendencies. She admits that politics is "not user-friendly," but says that it is now acceptable—and desirable—for women to compete as aggressively as men. As she has written in *The Journal of State Government* about women in politics: "Are we tough enough? Are we feminine enough? In the end we must answer [these questions] by simply forging ahead and doing what we believe must be done.... The opportunity to forge a connection between a desire for change and the achievement of actual change is what gives me the energy and determination to lead a political life."

All these women governors save one were elected. Rose Mofford, a Democrat known throughout Arizona as "Auntie Rose," became Governor of the state when Evan Mecham, the Republican Governor, was impeached in the spring of 1988. Although new to the office, Mofford is no stranger to politics—or to Arizonians.

Mofford, known for her beehive hairstyle, passion for golf, and her times as a softball player, had supervised state elections, managed state publications, and performed similar record-keeping duties as Secretary of State. She had held that elective post for ten years. Under Arizona law she was named acting governor when Mecham's impeachment process began and became governor when he was convicted.

Chapter **XII**

National Political Office

The routes to a top government post are as varied as the women who have followed them.

However, these women share certain attributes that have helped ensure their success. Those attributes include character itself—the strength to maintain their beliefs and uphold their convictions in the face of difficult odds. These winning women also have in common their toughness (even though it may not always be apparent); their ability to attract constituents, raise money, and establish a high profile; and a talent for working with the male establishment to get things done without compromising or losing sight of their particular agenda.

All of them have the backing of a support system, which in most cases consists of a husband and children or other family members (and, in one case, friends and political believers). Also, almost without exception, the women at the top in American politics have earned their posts by emerging victorious in at least one election rather than being appointed to office. (Even some who took office upon the death of their officeholder husband did so with special elections; a few of these have won reelection on their own strengths.)

Another characteristic these women share is plenty of time in the trenches of local and, especially, state politics. By the time they attained national office they had done their homework—often a great deal of homework because of the greater difficulties they encountered on the way up when compared to men holding similar offices. For the most part, these candidates have had to work harder to reach their goals than men.

COURTESY OFFICE OF NANCY KASSEBAUM
United States Senator Nancy L. Kassebaum.

Although it may not be altogether fair to say that all women members of Congress concentrate on apple-pie-and-motherhood, or home-and-hearth issues, they do tend as a group to pay more attention to matters of domestic policy than do their male counterparts. (Not all, however, are equally devoted to women's issues or feminism or the passage of the Equal Rights Amendment. And many have a great deal to say about world affairs and American foreign policy).

Another trait shared by most is the ability to listen, to hear what the people who may elect them think, fear, and want. And having listened, the women candidates have nearly all tended to make these "people issues" the cornerstones of their campaigns.

One further characteristic of successful female politicians, regardless of their agenda, does seem to be a fearlessness about rocking the boat and disturbing the status quo. It's not a guarantee of success (quite the opposite often happens!), but more than one national winner has displeased the Establishment but delighted the voters.

Tying all these characteristics together is another trait: consistency. That is not to say that male candidates change with the winds of fate more readily than women; it is rather that many of today's winning women are still promoting the same policies and working for the same goals at the national level that were their trademarks when they won city or state office.

Among the women at the top are conservative Republicans as well as liberal Democrats, with some female representation for every political stance in between. In this respect, they are like their male colleagues.

To see who some of these women are, let's begin with the quite different stories of our only two women Senators. Then we shall profile several women members of the U.S. House of Representatives.

If you were asked to name four American political families, you might mention the Kennedys, the Roosevelts, the Rockefellers, and perhaps the Scrantons. But would Nancy Kassebaum, the Republican Senator from Kansas, come to mind?

She would only if you knew the story of how she came to be one of the two women Senators (Barbara Mikulski is the other).

When Nancy Landon was born in 1932, her father, Alfred M. Landon, was running for Governor of Kansas. That bid was successful, but not so his 1936 candidacy for President, opposing Franklin D. Roosevelt. FDR swept into office for his second term; Landon carried only two states, neither of which was his home state.

Although Landon never again ran for office, he became a beloved political figure, especially in Kansas, until his death in 1987 at age 100. His daughter, Nancy, was surrounded by political talk and political personalities all through her growing-up years, and long afterward.

Although she majored in political science at the University of Kansas, it was not with the idea of becoming active politically. That was not to happen for more than twenty years.

Nancy Landon met her husband-to-be, John Philip Kassebaum, at college. They were married in 1955, and for the next twenty years, until they separated, Nancy Kassebaum led the life of a well-to-do homemaker and mother. She raised the children, became much involved in volunteer work, and paid little attention to politics. Had her marriage not broken up, her political career might never have gotten under way.

When she and her husband separated in 1975, she moved to Washington as an aide to Kansas Senator James Pearson. During her year in his office she learned the workings and the frustrations of national politics, and when the Senator announced that he would not seek reelection Kassebaum considered running for his seat.

She had quite a few things going for her. One was a fair amount of her own money to spend in the primary. Another was wide name recognition in a state where everyone—politically, at least—seems to know everyone else. (During the primary she was often accused of riding on her father's coattails. Her reply: "What better coattails could I ride on?") Through her college connections and her volunteer work, Nancy Kassebaum had formed a network of friends and workers throughout the state. Later, as she campaigned, there was hardly a Kansas town where she did not know at least one person.

A third and probably decisive advantage Kassebaum enjoyed was a strong sense of her own identity and capabilities. She reasoned that her extensive volunteer experience and her work as Senator Pearson's aide had equipped her to understand and respond to the needs of her future constituents. And she knew herself to be a highly capable manager and administrator.

When she had secured the Republican nomination she was opposed by former Congressman William Roy, a Democrat and a formidable campaigner who had nearly unseated Senator Robert

Dole in an earlier race. Kassebaum answered Roy's charges that she had not made a full disclosure of her finances by saying that her by-then separated husband was entitled to privacy. Kansans clearly preferred her quiet, low-key campaigning; she won with 54 percent of the vote.

At this writing, Senator Kassebaum is well into her second term. As she always has, she pays close attention to issues affecting her constituents. She also takes pleasure in the progress made by other women in politics. She applauds the fact that whereas when she first ran for office there was only one woman in the Kansas state senate, now there are six, many of whom worked for Kassebaum's campaign and entered politics themselves as a result.

Women in politics come from all sorts of backgrounds, but Nancy Landon Kassebaum is unusual: the daugher of a nationally known political figure who waited more than twenty years to achieve her political destiny.

When Barbara Mikulski won her Senate seat in 1986, she was far from a political neophyte. She had served five two-year terms as Representative from her home district, the predominantly Polish Highlandtown section of Baltimore. Before that her political career had begun in 1971 on the Baltimore City Council. And her college background was more or less related to politics: She had graduated from the University of Maryland School of Social Work.

This outspoken Senator from Maryland is proof positive that consistency— and paying full attention to the wishes of the voters in your district—will pay off politically. And it did so in a contest with a formidable opponent.

Even with her impressive credentials and lengthy experience, Barbara Mikulski did her homework well in the face of a challenge from a nationally recognized conservative Republican opponent. By staying true to the principles for which she was well known, Mikulski gained a decisive lead and became Maryland's first elected Democratic Senator in twenty-six years. (It was her second try for the seat.)

In winning, she set a few other records. She is the first Democratic woman to hold a Senate seat not previously held by her husband; the first Democratic woman to have served in both the House and Senate; and the first woman to win a statewide election in Maryland.

United States Senator Barbara A. Mikulski.

With the aid of polls and the willing services of old friends from her activist social worker days, Barbara Mikulski set out from her "safe" seat in the House to tackle the Senate race. She worked to earn support from business and civic leaders. Her supporters, mostly volunteer women including her own mother, worked hard for her candidacy, convinced that she would campaign vigorously for issues such as day care, the Equal Rights Amendment, and insurance reform. Mikulski drew as much financing as possible from the Women's Campaign Fund, the National Women's Political Caucus, and other feminist organizations, but feminism was far from her sole agenda. She fervently believes that women's issues are really family and people issues. She has said, "Making day care accessible is a business issue and a family issue." She considers such matters to be simple common sense.

In campaigning, she did not lose sight of long-standing local and regional issues: everything from revitalizing the Port of Baltimore to promoting the return of a National Football League team to her city, to an abiding concern for health care issues.

Her opponent for the Senate seat was another woman, Linda Chavez, a former staff director of the U.S. Commission on Civil Rights and a conservative Republican. The contrast between Chavez, who portrayed herself as a Reagan administration insider, and the outspoken liberal Democratic Congresswoman really gave the voters a choice. But even though President Reagan and Vice President Bush made appearances on Chavez' behalf, and even though she ran a considerable TV campaign, her slick commercials and criticism of Mikulski's liberal politics as belonging more in San Francisco than Maryland failed to impress the electorate. When Chavez posed with her husband and children in an effort to portray herself as the family candidate, the response from Barbara Mikulski (who is single) was typical: she declared the voters were her family. As Lavinia Edmunds wrote of the campaign in *Ms.* Magazine, "Mikulski kept her cool—or, rather, her warmth—throughout the mud-slinging." She won with 61 percent of the vote.

Her political agenda as Senator remains much as it was throughout her House career. She has been especially concerned with international issues: opposition to military and CIA activity in Honduras and to aid to the Nicaraguan Contras; divestment of South African business interests by American corporations; and verifiable nuclear disarmament. Of her career in the Senate, Mikulski says, "My issues will be economic growth for our country with equity, social justice, and world peace." Indeed, a tall order.

In profiling five 1988 women members of the U.S. House of Representatives, we find several things about them that are consistent. They all entered politics at the local level. They all worked extra-hard in their campaigning. Most are avowed feminists; all are staunch advocates of economic, "people" issues; and only one—Liz Patterson—came from a family background that included politics.

Illinois Congresswoman Lynn Martin was first elected in 1974 to the Winnebago County Board, with no political experience. Selected by local Republicans to run for the state legislature, she revitalized constituents who were planning not to vote in the aftermath of the Watergate scandals. From there her moves were upward, to state senate (1978) and to the U.S. Congress in 1980, where she stood for the seat vacated by Representative John Anderson when he decided to run for President. She won a five-candidate primary with 45 percent of the vote to be eligible for the general election.

Although she has said, "I didn't come to Washington with a mission," she has made it her goal to see exactly how government works—particularly how appropriations are managed, because she believes that money is what defines government. By knowing the rules, she feels better able to carry through what she believes to be worthy tasks of government and to limit those that she does not see as in the public interest.

Constance A. Morella, a Republican Congresswoman from Maryland, agrees with her party on most money matters but often takes a more liberal view on domestic issues, especially those affecting women.

Her political career began after she had raised nine children and had taught in a community college. During eight years in the Maryland state legislature, Morella fought hard for the Equal Rights Amendment and for stronger state child-support laws.

In seeking a House seat she continued to stress what she called "visceral issues"—equal pay for equal work and child care. During her campaign, she wore out six pairs of shoes, walking through her district at least four miles a day, waging a "people-to-people" campaign. Now in Washington, she continues to pursue these and similar issues on the national level.

Liz J. Patterson entered Congress in the 1987 term as a natural politician. A Democrat, she represents the fourth district of South Carolina, the state served by her late father, Senator Olin Johnston. But growing up attending political conventions and exchanging political talk did not mean that Patterson was able to start her climb to Congress from a higher vantage point than most women. She built her own record, working her way up from the Spartanburg County Council to the state senate, where she served from 1979 to 1987.

Having achieved visibility in her state senate career, Patterson emerged as the candidate of character, with straight answers to difficult campaign questions. In Washington, she continues to pursue her agenda—child care, welfare reform, health care, and education issues. Added to these is advocacy of reduced arms expenditures, with more emphasis on lower-cost conventional weapons. She is also fighting to maintain human services programs in the face of the Gramm-Rudman-Hollings deficit-reducing legislation.

Patricia Saiki, Republican Congresswoman from Hawaii, fits the personal composition of Hawaii's first district. She is an Asian-American in an area where nearly 37 percent of the residents are of Japanese descent, and where there are more women than men. However, Hawaii is a predominantly Democratic state, and how Pat Saiki reached Washington is an interesting story.

Saiki, like Connie Morella, is a former schoolteacher. She gained political recognition as a state representative for six years and a state senator for eight. An unsuccessful bid for lieutenant governor in 1982 added to her name recognition but did not improve her political fortunes.

These were revived by a successful period as state Republican chairperson. From this post Saiki aimed for the U.S. House of Representatives. She become one of the first congressional candidates to be targeted for funding by then Vice President George Bush—proving that men in power *will* support women candidates. To overcome the Democratic strength in Hawaii, she used the fact that the Republican Party, then in power nationally, needed to be better represented in Hawaii and to hear Hawaii's views. Strong party support, coupled with her moderate politics, brought her to victory.

Pat Saiki is a strong Equal Rights Amendment advocate, and will probably concentrate in Washington as she has at home on such issues as increased aid to education and improved care for the elderly.

To score an upset over a Republican incumbent in the 1986 Congressional election, Louise M. Slaughter, a liberal New York Democrat, designed her victory by—among other things—staging a series of "Hit the Streets with Louise" rallies. She literally walked through her district, talking to the voters. The fact that her opponent was against many federal programs that strongly affected their district didn't hurt her standing with the voters. He was not in favor of the Superfund to clean up toxic wastes, or of student loans, or grants for urban development. Slaughter stood for all those issues, and she won. Not surprisingly, she was backed by the National Women's Political Caucus.

This consistent supporter of women's issues has said, "The economic issues are ours...because we live them." In Washington, Slaughter is concerned with correcting the U.S. negative balance of trade. She is also working to improve job opportunities in New York, which she considers vital to the stability and future of the family. Thus she continues at the national level the work she began with her start in politics—three years in county legislature and four years in the state assembly. Slaughter's rise to high office has been consistent and impressive. She proves that starting at the bottom *can* take you to the top.

Chapter **XIII**

A Women's Hall of Fame

There aren't many members yet. But as women gain political prominence there will be more. Perhaps some of the women politicians we've already talked about will be among the most prominent political figures of the future.

It could be argued that every woman politician deserves to be in such a mythical hall of fame, but for now our entirely arbitrary designation goes to five women who have broken through to achieve distinction. They are a pioneering Congresswoman and Presidential candidate, America's senior woman member of Congress, the first woman to become a Justice of the U.S. Supreme Court, the first to be a candidate for Vice President, and the first to be elected head of state in a Western nation.

When you think of brilliant, trail-blazing women politicians, Shirley Chisholm immediately comes to mind. Chisholm, the now retired black Congresswoman from Brooklyn, New York, and at the time of her campaign the first woman since 1884 to run for the Presidency, has all the ingredients of a political pro. She is quick-witted, caring, fearless, and unyielding.

Mrs. Chisholm went from schoolteacher to Congresswoman, sharpening the qualities that would make her victorious against party candidates, political organizations, even against a conspiring Congress.

Although only 5' 2" and ninety-eight pounds, she was a formidable opponent. Her spirit and brilliance made up for her diminutive size. She edged past all contenders by "out-caring" and outsmarting them. She also proclaimed that she was "unbought and unbossed."

Shirley Chisholm showed this outsized determination early in

Former Congresswoman Shirley Chisholm

life. As a child she was a leader, and as a high school student she excelled academically. After a brief period of teaching, she put her skills to work at the Bureau of Child Guidance. She visited schools in various communities and encouraged their students to work hard for self-improvement. This community involvement led her onto a political path which she was to follow for many years.

Running for the New York State Legislature, Mrs. Chisholm won her seat with her breathtaking honesty and directness, overcoming vigorous opposition. During her tenure she managed to outrage the Democratic party by constantly bypassing the bosses. And she stayed in office one sure way—she worked harder than any other legislator, putting in long hours to acquaint herself with her district's problems.

Her next target was the U.S. House of Representatives. She won a seat on her record, and she was now about to establish some new ones. When the House establishment tried to put her on a committee for forestry and rural villages, she protested. Brooklyn was her territory—hardly a country setting! She was then reassigned to the Veterans' Affairs Committee, a place where she felt she could make a positive contribution.

Shirley Chisholm continued to fight for equal rights for women, the elimination of racism, and other minority issues. She took these issues right up to the Presidential primaries of 1972. And although George McGovern was to be the Democratic nominee, Chisholm made a respectable showing. Her run for the Presidency was the first in modern times for a woman, the first ever for a black.

Although no longer in politics and not in good health, Shirley Chisholm has set an example that will be followed one day by another woman—very possibly all the way to the Oval Office.

United States Representative Patricia Schroeder of Colorado is one of the higher-profile women in American elective politics. In 1972 as a thirty-two-year-old Harvard Law School graduate and political unknown, Mrs. Schroeder defeated a popular male incumbent in an under-financed campaign. She engineered an upset by focusing on antiwar and environmental issues. She is now the senior woman member of Congress, an attractive, straight-talking person who believes that her role in politics is to make a difference.

Schroeder believes strongly that women deserve more representation than they have now but concedes that it takes far more effort to run for office if you're a woman.

As she found out in 1988 when she tested the waters of Presidential politics, women candidates generally find it more difficult than men to solve the dual problems of attracting attention and raising money. While her brief bid did attract a reasonable amount of attention, her early primary campaign never generated the funds needed to sustain it.

Throughout her years in the House, Patricia Schroeder has held firmly to her concept of making a difference rather than simply going along with either the Democratic Party or her colleagues in the House. Although her relaxed, up-front style has not changed, she treats her responsibilities with a depth and intensity that are at odds with her apparently easygoing manner. Her agenda covers broad-based political issues rather than women's issues. She has said, "It's all too easy to become a kamikaze candidate, crashing and burning on one or two emotion-packed issues."

In this respect, although she is a steadfast feminist, she is also a realist, one who recognizes that not all women politicians support feminist issues. So Schroeder prefers to support other politicians on their stands on key issues rather than on their sex. She has often supported men whose positions she favored rather than their female opponents.

This position has not earned her universal acclaim, but on balance her consistent representation of her constituents and support of her own beliefs have probably put her ahead. When she received an honorary Doctor of Laws degree from the University of Pennsylvania in 1988, a University spokesperson said the degree was awarded in part because "...you have consistently fought for the rights of all people at home, while advocating enlightenment in United States foreign policy... As a member of the [House] Armed Services Committee, you questioned wasteful outlays from the start of your career and have spoken out in the current debate over United States policy in Central America. A forceful proponent of the Equal Rights Amendment [and] the Civil Rights Restoration Act, you have acted to bring pressure on the South African government to engage the majority of its people in open negotiation."

Speaking at a lecture series at Radcliffe College, Representative Schroeder addressed a subject that is important to her, women's place in history: "It's absolutely amazing how little of women's history we know. [Men] want us to believe that women arrived here on cruiseships and had their nails done every day....The truth is that not only George Washington was with the troops during those long, cold winters, but also Martha. Now, why don't we all know that?" She went on to say, "If we believe we weren't contributors, we get all apologetic, and everything starts to come unraveled." Similarly, she told of using women's presence as settlers on the western frontier—and therefore in a combat zone—as justifying her presence on the House Armed Services Committee. She related how she had researched the biographies of all Committee members to be familiar with their service records. Some had never served in the military. With this knowledge, she was able to respond to quite a few who asked, "How can you serve on this committee? You've never been in combat." To this she could reply, "Then you and I have a lot in common."

In discussing what had been expected of her as a Presidential contender, Schroeder said, "Everyone wanted me to do everything twice as fast and twice as well, or why was I even in it?" And when she talked about having cried during her withdrawal speech, she said, "All we read about for months was 'Did Pat Schroeder ruin women's chances for the next decade or even the next century by crying?' And then there were remarks like, 'I don't want anyone who cries to have a finger on the [nuclear] button.' Well, frankly," Schroeder continued, "I don't want anybody who *doesn't* cry to have a finger on the button."

She then focused on a deeper problem facing women in politics: acceptance. "Right now a man will let you in only if you can act like Madame Iron Britches. If a woman leader says, 'Yes, I am different and maybe I have a different prespective; what's wrong with having different opinions?' men go crazy. The challenge is to get them to accept women for both their abilities and their differences."

She also has a razor-sharp wit, which she uses politically and advises others to use. She told her Radcliffe listeners to, "Get your sense of humor sharpened up, and get your political skills sharpened up. The United States, thank goodness, is the kind of country where you can do it. And Martha Washington would say, 'It's about time.'"

In the 1992 campaign Representative Schroeder may well become the first woman to be a serious Presidential contender. "I think I will have to wait and see if our party will run on our very proud traditions," she commented after the Democratic Presidential defeat in 1988. Certainly her characteristics as a woman politician are exactly those needed by a successful President of the United States. To Patricia Schroeder, they include a firm, consistent grasp of domestic and worldwide issues, boundless determination, an unwavering energy level, a strong and flexible marriage (her husband, also an attorney, shifted his law practice to Washington when his wife won her House seat)—and, of course, money, or the ability to raise it.

As pressure continues to build for more women's representation at higher levels of government, this dynamic Representative's star may well rise still higher.

Sandra Day O'Connor is the first woman to be appointed an Associate Justice of the United States Supreme Court. Although this book highlights women in elective office, O'Connor joins the distinguished women in this chapter because many of her pre-Supreme Court years were spent in elective politics.

Sandra Day learned the values of hard work and self-reliance as a child on a working Arizona ranch. Later, she lived there only in summers while attending high school and majoring in law at Stanford University.

At a time when fewer than three percent of the university's law students were women, Sandra Day was not only accepted (at age sixteen) but later was honored by being named Editor of the Stanford Law Review. When she graduated with honors, however, no private law firm would hire her because of her sex, so she became a law clerk and later an Assistant District Attorney for the San Mateo (California) District Attorney's office. She credits this decision with setting her upon the course of public service that later became the principal area of her career.

She married and spent three years abroad working as a legal assistant for the U.S. Quartermaster Corps while her husband served in the Army. When the O'Connors returned to America, they settled in Phoenix. Both became partners in law firms. The demands of child-raising kept Sandra O'Connor from working full time and she later relinquished her law partnership.

Volunteer work and activism were her roles for a time. But a few years later her schedule made it possible for her to return to work and then to accept an appointment to the Arizona State Senate to fill an unexpired term. Later she was elected and reelected to her seat. On her reelection she was named the Republican Majority Leader, the first woman to hold that position in any state senate. During her Senate tenure she established her reputation for hard work, preparedness, and an evenhanded, tough-but-fair approach.

Her next elective office was as a Judge of the Arizona County Superior Court. Her work in this post resulted in her appointment to the Arizona State Court of Appeals. In 1979 came her first federal judicial appointment, to the Ninth U.S. Circuit Court of Appeals. It was from this post that she was named to the Supreme Court.

Besides being the first woman member of the Supreme Court, Justice O'Connor is one of the few Justices to have had only a relatively brief career in the federal judiciary, a fact that was brought out in her confirmation hearings before the U.S. Senate Judiciary Committee. Her supporters successfully contended that her many years as a state legislator and jurist had given her equal, if different, experience in dealing with legal issues.

Sandra Day O'Connor is a relatively young Supreme Court Justice. Her influence will undoubtedly grow in the years she may be expected to serve on the Court, a lifetime position. Is there a chance that, in the future, she might become the first woman Chief Justice?

On to another "first" in politics. The time was July 21, 1984. The place was the Democratic National Convention in San Francisco. The woman who stood at the speaker's platform acknowledged the delegates' cheers with the statement: "My name is Geraldine Ferraro. I stand before you to proclaim tonight: America is the land where dreams can come true for all of us."

The dream did not come true in the sense that Geraldine Ferraro, three-term Congresswoman from New York, actually did become the first woman Vice President of the United States. The 1984 Democratic ticket carried only one state and the District of Columbia. And certainly, the unfavorable publicity that surfaced during the campaign concerning her husband's business dealings and, later, her son's conviction on drug-selling charges made her future uncertain for a time. But Jeane Kirkpatrick, a high-profile politician in her own right, fully acknowledges Ferraro's breakthrough contribution. In Kirkpatrick's view, Ferraro fully proved the possibility of women holding high elective office. In the future the question will not be so much whether a woman can run for the second-highest office in the land (or even the number one post), but which woman should make the effort. The major problem, as all politically active women agree, is that there are not enough qualified women in elective office from which to choose possible winners. In the same context, Representative Patricia Schroeder of Colorado has said that the Vice Presidency "...is not an affirmative-action slot," and that "we [women] are not interested in a permanent spot as helpmate."

Ferraro herself is proud of the way she withstood the incredible pace of campaigning. It was, by her calculations, greater than that of any other candidate. She believes she handled herself well in some lengthy and very personal press conferences when her husband's real estate dealings became a campaign issue. She is proud, too, of the more than $6.1 million she raised on the campaign trail from men as well as women—more than was raised by her Presidential running mate, Walter Mondale.

In a 1988 interview with Margaret Wolf Freivogel of the St. Louis *Post-Dispatch*, Ferraro looked back on her nomination: "I don't even know how to express what it was like. The feeling of standing up there, knowing as you looked out on that sea of faces that they were just a small part of what was out there in this country. It wasn't Gerry Ferraro, it was the candidacy. I stood in for women. It was an incredible experience for me."

As for her life today, she believes that some of the unfavorable publicity arose because of her political stance, but she is philosophical. In the same interview, she said, "Nothing in life is 100 percent wonderful. You take the good with the bad. Life isn't fair. It's life. If you're an adult, you're able to handle it."

Like many women in politics, Ferraro had tremendous support from her family during her terms in Congress. She shuttled back and forth between her home district and Washington, at home only on weekends. During the week, her family maintained the household. And of course, they lent her full support during the hectic days and nights on the campaign trail in 1984.

The 1984 defeat returned Geraldine Ferraro to private life. She did not play an active role in the Democratic convention of 1988 but attended as a media commentator. One day she may resume the legal career from which she went to Congress. And as an Institute of Politics Fellow, she is still speaking out in her special, vigorous way on the issue of women in political life.

In a speech at Harvard Law School, Ferraro said, among other things, that women have taken key positions on candidates' election teams. "We're not talking about token women," she said. "We're talking about women sharing political power. Any time a woman runs for elected office it's like throwing a stone in a lake. The ripple effect is tremendous." However, she told her audience not to expect support from women's organizations "simply from biologically being a woman.... You will have to prove yourself first."

The progress of women in elective politics, she said, "will happen in time, but it is not just a matter of time." She looks forward to the time when "fewer women will be making history, and more women will be making policy."

One woman to whom policymaking is almost routine is one of the world's most successful, enduring political leaders of either sex. She is Margaret Thatcher, the Conservative Party Prime Minister of Great Britain. For the majority of Britons who keep returning her to office, she is a symbol of her country's renewed vitality. For American women, she proves that national leadership is not exclusively a male prerogative.

Margaret Thatcher embodies all the qualities needed for women who plan to enter politics. She is ambitious, idealistic, tough-minded, and full of energy. And like other farsighted political women, she is a strong policymaker. This attribute feeds the sense of power she covets.

Utterly fearless, the "Iron Lady" is willing to take unpopular stands, including resisting the demands of British labor unions and opposing the European Community (the Common Market) when she feels their positions threaten Britain's new-found stability.

Margaret Thatcher is the longest-reigning British Prime Minister of the twentieth century. Although she has many ardent supporters, she also has some vocal detractors. Many criticize her for her policies; others, for her aloofness and her single-minded determination to see things done her way.

One day America may have a woman Chief Executive. Like

Margaret Thatcher, she will have her supporters and detractors. And like Thatcher, she will rise above dissension and move onward. Self-confidence in the face of opposition is one key to effective governing.

Chapter **XIV**

Nonelective Politics

This book has concentrated on how women can be elected to public office, but the ballot box is not the only way to a career in politics or government. Federal civil service jobs dealing with politics and appointive positions in national and international affairs employ great numbers of people. Lobbying, women's political organizations, volunteering, special-interest groups, the media, and other activities related to the public are all routes to political experience. This chapter touches briefly on some of these nonelective areas.

For students in high school, just out of high school, or in college, volunteering is a great introduction to politics. Marc Schuhl, a high school senior, covers the phones for Lois Hagarty, a Pennsylvania State Representative. He enjoys the opportunity to participate in politics, serving both Mrs. Hagarty and her constituents. Later, Marc may volunteer in other ways, perhaps even as a delegate to a national political convention.

Political candidates would never be able to project their views, address campaign issues, or build voter turnout without the volunteers who put their hearts, minds, and *time* into making the democratic way a success. Women of all ages address envelopes, make phone calls, distribute literature, and work at the polls. They are the glue that holds a campaign together. And you, the reader, are never too young to volunteer for this sort of activity. Get in touch with the local organization of the political party you favor or the office of the candidate you wish to support.

Volunteer and paid jobs can be found with special-interest groups. These range in scope from broad-based organizations addressing women's issues such as NOW (the National Organization for Women) or single-issue groups such as Women for Disarmament. Endless other focus groups concentrate on the environment, senior citizens' rights, and other public concerns. Here, too, volunteering is as easy as contacting the organization's nearest chapter or talking to a member.

Volunteering often leads to an unexpected commitment. Young or older women only mildly interested in some political area may find their involvement setting the course for their lives. The members of NOW and other women's rights organizations have brought women into the twenty-first century. The NOW lobbyists work behind the scenes to influence legislators in favor of issues that benefit women. The organization also supports women candidates who are sympathetic to its views. Other organizations such as the National Women's Political Caucus carry great power, too. Put together, these groups have great influence at all political levels, right up to the top.

In addition to a continual need for volunteers, such organizations usually have paid jobs available, usually for people with strong fund-raising, executive, and administrative skills. The late Frances Perkins is an excellent example. For young people, Miss Perkins is a figure of the past. But she is well worth mentioning because she represents a milestone in women's politics.

Although she never ran for elective office, Frances Perkins was one of the most influential American political figures of this century. She was the first woman to hold Cabinet rank in the federal government. She served as Secretary of Labor throughout the administration of President Franklin D. Roosevelt, from 1933 to 1945.

"Madame Secretary," as she was usually addressed, brought to this highly sensitive position a wide-ranging background in social activism, coupled with strong executive and administrative skills. She was the unwavering champion of working people (not just of women who worked), of the poor, and of all those she felt were not treated fairly in American society.

Her experience with the poor in the settlement houses of Philadelphia and Chicago and her strong reaction to New York's Triangle factory fire drove her to strive for social legislation and worker safety laws for the state of New York. These causes set the stage for her social action at the national level.

Under Governors Smith and Roosevelt of New York, Miss Perkins was the state labor department administrator who worked for twelve years (the last four as department head) to assure the passage of protective legislation. When Governor Roosevelt became President Roosevelt, he expected Frances Perkins to work for similar legislation nationally. His trust was not misplaced.

Although most of the ideas she favored for national legislation were neither new nor original with her, she was the driving force behind enactment. She deserves much of the credit for such landmark New Deal legislation as the 40-hour workweek, the minimum wage, and the entire concept of Social Security. Before the Roosevelt administration, none of these laws that we take for granted existed nationally.

Even though the purpose of these laws was to help all Americans, including business, to recover from the effects of the Depression of the early 1930s, Frances Perkins had to overcome considerable resistance in and out of politics to have the legislation passed by Congress. Many corporate heads and even some labor leaders were against it, and against Perkins. Unfortunately, much of this resistance was to a woman performing what by tradition had been a man's job. Although criticism of her policies and the fact that she was a woman plagued her throughout her career (not helped by her often prickly relations with the press), she never wavered in the face of challenge and rarely replied to her detractors.

She never retired, either. After President Roosevelt's death, she resigned from the Department of Labor but performed other government work. She also wrote the first biography of President Roosevelt, *The Roosevelt I Knew*, and lectured on sociopolitical issues at several universities, notably Cornell, almost until her death in 1965 at the age of eighty-five.

As the first woman member of a President's Cabinet, Frances Perkins blazed a trail, but it was not until years later that other women followed. The most recent is Elizabeth Hanford Dole, Secretary of Transportation during the Reagan administration and—following Miss Perkins—Secretary of Labor in the Bush Cabinet.

Another group of "appointees" who wield strong influence are lobbyists. Special-interest groups from NOW to handgun control and industries from real estate to petroleum employ lobbyists. The term "lobbying" arose from the fact that, in earlier times, those wishing to affect legislation pleaded their causes to legislators in the lobbies and corridors outside the House and Senate (some believe the term originated with the British Houses of Parliament). These days lobbyists wine and dine legislators and try to make strong cases for the organizations they represent. Successful lobbyists are well paid and are a decidedly important part of politics.

Lobbying plays no part in the operation of one strictly volunteer organization devoted to getting people—especially women—involved in politics. That is the League of Women Voters. The League is basically an information-dispensing organization; it does not support or oppose specific candidates, but it does state the views of both sides in political contests. The League also works to raise the collective political consciousness; it has in recent elections organized and conducted nationally televised debates by the leading Presidential candidates. The League conducts similar kinds of consciousness-raising for voters in all types of contests, from citywide to nationwide. It compiles candidates' voting records and positions on the issues and sees that these are published in newspaper supplements and handbills before election time. It also creates county government handbooks that help the voters to find local government services and sources of help.

Approximately one-third of federal civil service jobs today go to women college graduates, and the proportion is slowly rising. Almost every "civilian" job has an equivalent in the federal government, so a great many of these jobs are not politically oriented. However, those that are related to federal cabinet posts (State Department; Foreign Service; Health and Human Services, Education, etc.) can be considered part of the American political system.

Most federal jobs (and all that are covered by civil service) are secured through competitive examinations. Since the formation in 1962 of President Kennedy's Commission on the Status of Women, sex may not be considered in hiring for federal employment, unless the particular job can be filled only by one sex. (Interestingly, the executive order eliminating sex discrimination in federal hiring did not grow out of the Kennedy Commission; it preceded it by exactly 100 years. The original order was signed during the Civil War, when women were needed to fill government jobs and were not paid equally with men. When the war was over, the policy was conveniently forgotten. The Kennedy Commission reinstated the original requirement.)

Although equal pay for equal work is the law in federal employment, women on the average do tend to earn less than men in government work because they hold lower-level jobs than men do.

The positions most closely related to active politics are those of assistants and legislative aides to members of Congress. Each member of the House and Senate has his or her own staff. In addition to a legislative aide with knowledge of the lawmaking process, the staff can include a press aide to deal with the media, caseworkers who reply to mail from constituents, and support staffs in Washington and at offices in the Senator's or Representative's home area. Many of these Washington staff people come from the legislator's home state or district. Many staff members earned their job by working for the officeholder at election time. Another avenue is through temporary work during high school or college summer vacations; such internships may lead to full-time employment later.

Although judges are often elected, this is not universally so. Sandra Day O'Connor did run for various offices, but Supreme Court Justice was not among them. That is an appointive post, with the candidate selected by the President and confirmed (or rejected) by the U.S. Senate. Many other federal judges are also appointed.

Many posts in the American diplomatic corps are appointive as well. All ambassadors to foreign countries are selected by the President. Like Cabinet officers, ambassadors may choose the members of their personal staffs—another area in which women may serve as capably as men. However, ambassadorships are still very much male-dominated. Since they are often considered semiceremonial posts, they are awarded to the faithful (often the big contributors) of the party in power; however, many ambassadors—and nearly all of the permanent overseas diplomatic corps and embassy staffs—are career civil servants. Again, with a higher proportion of women than ever being hired for civil service posts, work overseas may well be part of your nonelective political future.

Not all appointive jobs are in Washington or at the national level. Similar work may be found in state capitals in the offices of state legislators. Since these legislators all maintain offices in their home communities, it may be possible to work in state government right in your own hometown.

It's possible to be in the thick of politics on the staff of a local politician such as a mayor or member of a city council. There are positions, too, in county government as an aide or administrative assistant to a county commissioner. And of course, political parties at all levels have paid as well as volunteer jobs.

Women now run national as well as local election campaigns. Several were highly visible during the 1988 Presidential campaign. Michael Dukakis's campaign manager was a woman. George Bush's campaign co-chairperson and his policy adviser were both female. Women at the top in national compaigns no longer appear out of place as they tackle one of the most demanding jobs possible—getting their candidates elected.

Other related career areas include working for a polling or opinion research organization, becoming an election specialist or candidate "packager" in the advertising business, or becoming a media person who concentrates on politics. Such posts can range from the hard-earned jobs of national political TV or magazine and news service reporting through the state government structure to the local level—to reporting on the activities (and the shenanigans!) of county, town, township, or school board for a local newspaper. The needs are the same no matter how large or small the reportage area: a thorough knowledge of who's who on the political scene, a firm grasp of the issues, and a talent for accurate, lively communication.

As you can see from this brief summary, there are many ways to be a part of politics without ever having to make a speech, hold a press conference, or debate an opponent.

Chapter **XV**

Where Do You Go from Here?

The answer to that question is, of course, entirely up to you. With American politics more open to women than ever before, your options for a career in this area are many. Exercising those options, however, won't necessarily be easy.

The Eagleton Institute at Rutgers University emphasizes the political realities in its woman-awareness courses, but you need not wait until college to be aware of five issues raised in its classes. They are important to any political career decision you make:

1. *It's tough to be a woman in politics.* It doesn't matter what your political or personal style might be; you will find roadblocks as a woman candidate. Whether you are quiet or outspoken, easygoing or intense, and regardless of your political persuasion (Republican or Democrat, liberal or conservative), the road can be hard. After all, the vast majority of political elective offices are still held by men. Even the most experienced women are looked upon as newcomers, as unqualified, even as challengers who threaten traditional ways of doing things. Women have to be far more convincing than men, even among women. The very fact that a woman is running for office is no guarantee that she will get the votes of other women.

2. *Political women have strong bonds.* They do because they have to. Women today are fully aware that they must work collectively. Many women have put other women over the top politically. They do this by joining forces to help women win political office, and women's organizations support the interests and agendas of the officeholders. Thus you could become politically involved by working with an activist group or a professional or civic organiza-

tion that supports the nomination and election of women candidates. And one day you may become an active politician yourself.

3. *Political women make a difference.* As you have read in this book, that is the primary belief of U.S. Representative Patricia Schroeder of Colorado and of countless other women who hold political office. Women believe, rightly, that their experiences and approaches to political issues are often very different from those of men. These differing perspectives can make women desirable alternatives in the eyes of voters if the differences can be made clear.

4. *The past ten years have seen tremendous change.* In this case, "change" means large increases in the active roles women have played in elective politics. More than three times as many women now hold political office as did ten years ago. These women now have some share of political power. This is truer on the local and regional level than it is nationally, however. To date, the higher the rung on the political ladder, the less the proportion of women. Jeane Kirkpatrick has said that Geraldine Ferraro's 1984 Vice Presidential candidacy set the stage for the future. It may not be too many years before a woman runs for the Presidency—this time as a major party candidate.

5. *The work has barely begun.* While it is true that in recent years women have moved onto the political stage, they have yet with rare exception to take stage center and gain the spotlight. Relatively few women hold office. Because their numbers are so small, women officeholders rarely hold key power positions. In fact, a great many caucuses, discussion groups, and political circles include no women at all. Women have had to create their own roles far more than have men. Men can usually count on a network of their peers to help achieve mutual goals. As women increase their numbers, their own networking will begin to give them a greater degree of collective power, and campaign money.

We would add a sixth point to the Eagleton Institute's observations: *Women are entering politics earlier in life.* This fact was covered in Chapter V, but its significance to women makes it worth repeating. Growing numbers of women are becoming politically active long before their children are grown. Yes, it takes a strong support system (which may be a code phrase for "understanding husband"), but more and more young women like State Representative Frances Weston of Pennsylvania are doing it.

The implications of this trend are important to you. It may well be that, with a start as early as high school and solid political training in college, you to could embark on a career in elective politics before too many years have passed.

Appendix I

Women in Public Office

We are indebted for the following statistical material to the Center for the American Woman and Politics, National Information Bank on Women in Public Office, Eagleton Institute of Politics, Rutgers University.

**SUMMARY OF WOMEN CANDIDATES
FOR SELECTED OFFICES: 1968–1988**
(Major Party Nominees)

Selected Statewide Elective Executives and State Legislators

Year	Governor	Lt. Governor	Secretary of State	State Auditor	State Treasurer	State Legislator
1974	3(1D,2R)	4(1D,3R)	14(6D,8R)	5(3D,2R)	10(8D,2R)	1125
1976	2(2D,0R)	1(0D,1R)	3(0D,3R)	0	6(3D,3R)	1258
1978	1(1D,0R)	9(6D,3R)	16(9D,7R)	2(2D,0R)	10(6D,4R)	1348
1980	0	3(2D,1R)	4(1D,3R)	3(2D,1R)	3(2D,1R)	1451
1982	2(2D,0R)	7(4D,3R)	14(7D,7R)	1(1D,0R)	10(6D,4R)	1643
1984	1(1D,0R)	6(4D,2R)	6(4D,2R)	4(2D,2R)	1(1D,0R)	1756
1986	8(3D,5R)	11(6D,5R)	21(14D,7R)	6(4D,2R)	11(7D,4R)	1813
1988	2(2D,0R)	2(1D,1R)	3(2D,1R)	2(0D,2R)	2(1D,1R)	1859

U.S. Congress

Year	Senate	House
1968	1(1D,0R)	19(12D,7R)
1970	1(0D,1R)	25(15D,10R)
1972	2(0D,2R)	32(24D,8R)
1974	3(2D,1R)	44(30D,14R)
1976	1(1D,0R)	54(34D,20R)
1978	2(1D,1R)	46(27D,19R)
1980	5(2D,3R)	52(27D,25R)
1982	3(1D,2R)	55(27D,28R)
1984	10(6D,4R)	65(30D,35R)
1986	6(3D,3R)	64(30D,34R)
1988	2(0D,2R)	59(33D,26R)

WOMEN CANDIDATES FOR STATE LEGISLATURES: 1986 AND 1988
Party and Seat Summary

STATE SENATE AND STATE HOUSE

Total	
1986	1988
1813	1859

1986		1988
846	Incumbent	891
556	Challenger	577
411	Open Seat	391

	Democrats		Republicans		Nonpartisans*	
	1986	1988	1986	1988	1986	1988
Total	975	1050	833	800	5	9
Incumbent	456	512	388	375	2	4
Challenger	283	312	272	265	1	0
Open Seat	236	226	173	160	2	5

STATE SENATE

Total	
1986	1988
261	302

1986		1988
107	Incumbent	140
86	Challenger	105
68	Open Seat	57

	Democrats		Republicans		Nonpartisans*	
	1986	1988	1986	1988	1986	1988
Total	137	167	119	126	5	9
Incumbent	63	76	42	60	2	4
Challenger	35	63	50	42	1	0
Open Seat	39	28	27	24	2	5

STATE HOUSE

	Total		Democrats		Republicans	
	1986	1988	1986	1988	1986	1988
Total	1552	1557	838	883	714	674
Incumbent	739	751	393	436	346	315
Challenger	470	472	248	249	222	223
Open Seat	343	334	197	198	146	136

STATE SENATE AND STATE HOUSE HOLDOVERS

	Total		State Senate		State House	
	1986	1988	1986	1988	1986	1988
Total	97	150	68	80	29	70
Democrats	56	109	34	51	22	58
Republicans	34	38	28	26	6	12
Nonpartisans	6	3	6	3	NA	NA
Independent	1	0	0	0	1	0

---

* The Nebraska legislature is unicameral; legislators are elected on a nonpartisan basis.

APPENDIX 1: WOMEN IN PUBLIC OFFICE   111

WOMEN CANDIDATES FOR STATE LEGISLATURES 1988

State	Total Legislature Cand.	Total Won	Total HO+	Senate Cand. D	Senate Cand. R	Senate Won D	Senate Won R	Senate HO+ D	Senate HO+ R	House Cand. D	House Cand. R	House Won D	House Won R	House HO+ D	House HO+ R
AL	0		8	0	0	0	0	0	1	0	0	0	0	7	0
AK	18		2	2	3			1	1	7	6			0	0
AR	8	8	2	0	0	0	0	2	0	7	1	7	1	0	0
AZ	47	27	0	7	7	2	3	0	0	16	16	9	13	0	0
CA	32		1	6	3			1	0	14	9			0	0
CO	40		2	3	5			0	2	17	15	19	15	0	0
CT	74	41	0	5	7	4	3	0	2	30	32	2	4	0	0
DE	11	7	3	1	1	1	0	1	2	4	5	7	8	0	0
FL	32	18	7	2	3	2	1	4	3	14	13	18	4	0	0
GA	36	24	0	1	3	1	1	0	0	25	7	9	2	0	0
HI	24	16	2	2	5	2	3	2	0	11	6	5	17	0	0
ID	47	31	0	9	5	6	3	0	1	14	19	9	12	0	0
IL	57	32	1	10	6	6	5	0	1	18	23	5	6	0	0
IN	33	20	2	6	5	5	4	1	1	12	10	13	6	0	0
IA	38	23	2	3	4	2	2	1	1	17	14	16	17	0	0
KS	71	42	0	9	7	5	4	0	0	33	22	0	0	0	0
KY	10		1	0	0	0	0	1	0	6	4			0	0
LA	0	0	4	0	0	0	0	0	0	0	0	0	0	4	0
ME	96	0	0	8	7	0	0	0	0	39	42	0	0	29	4
MD	0	0	39	0	0	0	0	6	0	0	0	0	0	0	0
MA	40		0	4	1			0	0	24	11			0	0
MI	48	20	2	0	0	0	0	1	1	30	18	12	8	0	0
MN	48		9	1	1			6	3	28	18			0	0

WOMEN CANDIDATES FOR STATE LEGISLATURES 1988 (cont.)

State	Total Legislature Cand.	Won	HO+	State Senate Candidates D	R	Won D	R	HO+ D	R	State House Candidates D	R	Won D	R	HO+ D	R
MS	0	0	10	0	0	0	0	2	1	0	0	0	0	7	0
MO	36	28	1	1	2	0	1	1	1	21	12	19	8	0	0
MT	41		2	4	2			2	0	23	12			0	0
NE	9		3	9NP*				3NP*		UNICAMERAL					
NV	30		0	3	2			0	0	10	15			0	0
NH	207	136	0	3	5	2	4	0	0	106	92	49	81	2	6
NJ	0		11	0	0	0	0	2	1	0	0	0	0	2	0
NM	26		0	4	6			0	0	8	8			0	0
NY	56		0	9	3			0	0	23	21			0	0
NC	36		0	4	2			0	0	20	10			0	0
ND	55	22	2	3	1	2	1	1	1	27	23	10	9	0	0
OH	33		1	2	2			1	0	22	7			0	0
OK	18		2	5	1			1	1	7	5			0	0
OR	32		4	4	1			3	1	17	10			0	0
PA	40		1	4	0			1	0	19	17			0	0
RI	31		0	5	8			0	0	12	6			0	0

SC	22		0	2	2			0	0	12	6			0	0
SD	39	21	0	8	4	6	2	0	0	17	10	6	7	0	0
TN	19		0	2	1			0	0	8	8			0	0
TX	25		2	0	1			2	0	17	7			0	0
UT	22		1	1	1			1	0	12	8			0	0
VT	80	55	0	7	3	6	0	0	0	40	30	26	23	0	0
VA	0	0	14	0	0	0	0	2	1	0	0	0	0	9	2
WA	68	38	4	5	4	3	3	2	2	32	27	22	10	0	0
WV	41	23	1	4	1	4	1	1	0	21	15	16	2	0	0
WI	47	33	2	3	1	1	1	0	2	25	18	18	13	0	0
WY	36	20	2	5	0	2	0	2	0	16	15	7	11	0	0
TOTAL	1859	**	150	167	126	**	**	51	26	881	673	**	**	58	12
				9NP*				3NP*							

+HO = Holdover
*NP = Nonpartisan
**Many results not available at time of printing.
In AL and MD, where all legislators are elected for four-year terms, there were no state legislative races in 1988. In LA, MS, NJ, and VA all legislative races are held in odd-numbered years; hence no state legislative races were held in 1988.

WOMEN CANDIDATES FOR CONGRESS AND STATEWIDE OFFICES: 1988 ELECTION RESULTS

US CONGRESS

As a result of the 1988 elections, the number of women serving in Congress will reach a record high of **27**. In 1989 in the 101st Congress, **2** (ID, IR) women will serve in the Senate and **25** (14D, 11R) women will serve in the House. Women will hold **5%** of the 535 available seats in Congress — **2%** of all Senate seats and **5.8%** of all House seats.

US Senate
2 candidates (2R) — **0** winners
(1 challenger; 1 open seat)
2 holdovers (1D, 1R)

US House of Representatives
59 candidates (33D, 26R) — **25** winners (14D, 11R)

	Total Candidates	Winners	Democrats Candidates	Winners	Republicans Candidates	Winners
Total	59	25	33	14	26	11
Incumbent	23	23	12	12	11	11
Challenger	32	1	17	1	15	0
Open Seat	4	1	4	1	0	0

STATEWIDE ELECTIVE EXECUTIVES

As a result of the 1988 elections, **45**, or **13.6%**, of the 330 statewide elective executive officials in 1989 will be women. The **45** (32D, 12R, 1NP[+]) officials will include: 3 governors, 4 lieutenant governors, 1 attorney general, 11 secretaries of state, 10 treasurers, 6 auditors, 4 superintendents of public instruction, 1 commissioner of education, 1 commissioner of labor, 1 commissioner of agriculture, 1 tax commissioner, 1 corporation commissioner, and 1 public utilities commissioner. (These figures do not include women appointed to state cabinet-level positions or officials elected to executive posts by the legislature.)

Statewide Elective Executives
23 candidates (11D, 11R, 1NP) — **11** winners (6D, 4R, 1NP)
34 holdovers (26D, 8R)

	Total Candidates	Winners	Democrats Candidates	Winners	Republicans Candidates	Winners
Total	23*	11*	11	6	11	4
Incumbent	5	4	4	3	1	1
Challenger	11	3	3	0	8	3
Open Seat	7*	4*	4	3	2	0

*includes 1 nonpartisan election
[+]NP = nonpartisan election

WOMEN CANDIDATES 1988: ELECTION RESULTS

State	Office	District	Candidate	Seat*	Race**	GE Results
HI	US Sen.		Maria Hustace (R)	C	W	Lost
WI	US Sen.		Susan Engeleiter (R)	O	W	Lost
AZ	US Rep.	05	Judy Belcher (D)	C	W	Lost
CA	US Rep.	05	Nancy Pelosi (D)	I	W	Won
CA	US Rep.	06	Barbara Boxer (D)	I	W	Won
CA	US Rep.	07	Jean Last (R)	C	W	Lost
CA	US Rep.	12	Anna Eshoo (D)	O	W	Lost
CA	US Rep.	14	Patricia Malberg (D)	C	W	Lost
CA	US Rep.	15	Carol Harner (R)	C	W	Lost
CA	US Rep.	20	Lita Reid (D)	C	W	Lost
CA	US Rep.	40	Lida Lenney (D)	O	W	Lost
CO	US Rep.	01	Patricia Schroeder (D)	I	W	Won
CO	US Rep.	01	Joy Wood (R)	C	W	Lost
CO	US Rep.	06	Martha Ezzard (D)	C	W	Lost
CT	US Rep.	01	Barbara B. Kennelly (D)	I	W	Won
CT	US Rep.	06	Nancy L. Johnson (R)	I	W	Won
FL	US Rep.	08	C. Bette Wimbish (D)	C	B	Lost
HI	US Rep.	01	Mary Bitterman (D)	C	W	Lost
HI	US Rep.	01	Patricia Saiki (R)	I	AP	Won
ID	US Rep.	01	Jeanne Givens (D)	C	NA	Lost
IL	US Rep.	07	Cardiss Collins (D)	I	B	Won
IL	US Rep.	13	Evelyn Craig (D)	C	W	Lost
IL	US Rep.	16	Lynn M. Martin (R)	I	W	Won
IN	US Rep.	04	Jill Long (D)	C	W	Lost
IN	US Rep.	05	Patricia Williams (R)	C	W	Lost
KS	US Rep.	03	Jan Meyers (R)	I	W	Won
LA	US Rep.	02	Corinne "Lindy" Boggs (D)	I	W	Won
LA	US Rep.	08	Faye Williams (D)	C	B	Lost
MA	US Rep.	04	Debra Tucker (R)	C	W	Lost
MD	US Rep.	02	Helen D. Bentley (R)	I	W	Won
MD	US Rep.	06	Beverly B. Byron (D)	I	W	Won
MD	US Rep.	08	Constance A. Morella (R)	I	W	Won
ME	US Rep.	02	Olympia Snowe (R)	I	W	Won
MI	US Rep.	02	Lana Pollack (D)	C	W	Lost
MO	US Rep.	05	Mary Ellen Lobb (R)	C	W	Lost
NE	US Rep.	03	Virginia Smith (R)	I	W	Won
NJ	US Rep.	04	Betty Holland (D)	C	W	Lost
NJ	US Rep.	05	Marge Roukema (R)	I	W	Won
NM	US Rep.	03	Cecilia M. Salazar (R)	C	H	Lost
NV	US Rep.	01	Lucille Luck (R)	C	W	Lost
NV	US Rep.	02	Barbara Vucanovich (R)	I	W	Won
NY	US Rep.	17	Myrna Albert (R)	C	W	Lost
NY	US Rep.	20	Nita Lowey (D)	C	W	Won
NY	US Rep.	22	Eleanor Burlingham (D)	C	W	Lost
NY	US Rep.	27	Rosemary Pooler (D)	O	W	Lost
NY	US Rep.	30	Louise M. Slaughter (D)	I	W	Won
OH	US Rep.	09	Marcy Kaptur (D)	I	W	Won
OH	US Rep.	11	Margaret Mueller (R)	C	W	Lost
OH	US Rep.	14	Loretta Lang (R)	C	W	Lost
OH	US Rep.	20	Mary Rose Oakar (D)	I	W	Won

116 CAREERS FOR WOMEN IN POLITICS

State	Office	District	Candidate	Seat*	Race**	GE Results
RI	US. Rep.	02	Ruth Morgenthau (D)	C	W	Lost
RI	US. Rep.	02	Claudine Schneider (R)	I	W	Won
SC	US. Rep.	04	Elizabeth J. Patterson (D)	I	W	Won
TN	US. Rep.	03	Marilyn Lloyd (D)	I	W	Won
TX	US. Rep.	07	Diane Richards (D)	C	W	Lost
TX	US. Rep.	26	Jo Ann Reyes (D)	C	H	Lost
WA	US. Rep.	03	Jolene Unsoeld (D)	O	W	Won
WA	US. Rep.	05	Marlyn Derby (R)	C	W	Lost
WI	US. Rep.	02	Ann Haney (R)	C	W	Lost
WI	US. Rep.	05	Helen Barnhill (R)	C	B	Lost
WV	US. Rep.	04	Marianne Brewster (R)	C	W	Lost
MO	Governor		Betty Hearnes (D)	C	W	Lost
VT	Governor		Madeleine Kunin (D)	I	W	Won
MT	Lt. Gov.		Barbara Skelton (D)	O	W	Lost
ND	Lt. Gov.		Donna Nalewaja (R)	C	W	Lost
OR	Sec. St.		Barbara Roberts (D)	I	W	Won
RI	Sec. St.		Kathleen Connell (D)	I	W	Lost
RI	Sec. St.		Mary Lukens (R)	C	W	Won
RI	Atty. Gen.		Kathleen Voccola (R)	C	W	Lost
NC	St. Treas.		Nancy Lake Coward (R)	C	W	Lost
PA	St. Treas.		Catherine Baker Knoll (D)	O	W	Won
MT	Auditor		Andrea Bennett (R)	I	W	Won
PA	Auditor		Barbara Hafer (R)	C	W	Won
IN	Sup. Pub. In		Mary Pettersen (D)	C	W	Lost
MT	Sup. Pub. In		Barbara Foster (R)	O	W	Lost
MT	Sup. Pub. In		Nancy Keenan (D)	O	W	Won
WA	Sup. Pub. In		Judith Billings (NP)***	O	W	Won
ND	Comm. Ag.		Sarah Vogel (D)	O	W	Won
DE	Comm. Ins.		Ruth Matruder (R)	C	W	Lost
ND	Comm. Ins.		Margaret Bushee (R)	C	W	Lost
ND	Tax Comm.		M.K. Heidi Heitkamp (D)	I	W	Won
AZ	Corp. Comm.		Kate Lehman (D)	C	W	Lost
NM	Corp. Comm.		Jannie McDaniel (R)	O	W	Lost
SD	Pub. Uti. Co		Laska Schoenfelder (R)	C	W	Won

*Seat: I = Incumbent; C = Challenger; O = Open Seat
**Race: W = White; B = Black; H = Hispanic; AP = Asian Pacific; NA = Native American
***Party: NP = Nonpartisan election

APPENDIX 1: WOMEN IN PUBLIC OFFICE 117

WOMEN OFFICEHOLDERS NOT UP FOR REELECTION IN 1988

In addition to the candidates who won in 1988, the following women will serve in 1989:

U.S. Senate — 2 (1D, 1R)

State	Office	Name	Race*
KS	US Sen.	Nancy Kassebaum (R)	W
MD	US Sen.	Barbara A. Mikulski (D)	W

Statewide Elected Executives — 34 (26D, 8R)

AZ	Governor	Rose Mofford (D)	W
NE	Governor	Kay A. Orr (R)	W
IA	Lt. Gov.	Jo Ann Zimmerman (D)	W
MA	Lt. Gov.	Evelyn Murphy (D)	W
MI	Lt. Gov.	Martha Griffiths (D)	W
MN	Lt. Gov.	Marlene Johnson (DFL)	W
CA	Sec. St.	March Fong Eu (D)	AP
CO	Sec. St.	Natalie Meyer (R)	W
CT	Sec. St.	Julia H. Tashjian (D)	W
IA	Sec. St.	Elaine Baxter (D)	W
MN	Sec. St.	Joan Anderson Growe (DFL)	W
NM	Sec. St.	Rebecca Vigil-Giron (D)	H
NV	Sec. St.	Frankie Sue Del Papa (D)	W
SD	Sec. St.	Joyce Hazeltine (R)	W
WY	Sec. St.	Kathy Karpan (D)	W
VA	Atty. Gen.	Mary Sue Terry (D)	W
AR	St. Treas.	Jimmie Lou Fisher (D)	W
CO	St. Treas.	Gail S. Schoettler (D)	W
DE	St. Treas.	Janet Rzewnicki (R)	W
ID	St. Treas.	Lydia Justice Edwards (R)	W
IN	St. Treas.	Marjorie O'Laughlin (R)	W
KS	St. Treas.	Joan Finney (D)	W
LA	St. Treas.	Mary Landrieu (D)	W
OH	St. Treas.	Mary Ellen Withrow (D)	W
TX	St. Treas.	Ann W. Richards (D)	W
AL	Auditor	Jan Cook (D)	W
AR	Auditor	Julia Hughes Jones (D)	W
IN	Auditor	Ann G. DeVore (R)	W
MO	Auditor	Margaret Kelly (R)	W
FL	Comm. Educ.	Betty Castor (D)	W
AZ	Sup. Pub. In.	C. Diane Bishop (D)	W
WY	Sup. Pub. In.	Lynn Simons (D)	W

OR	Comm. Labor	Mary Roberts (D)	W
AZ	Corp. Comm.	Marcia Weeks (D)	W

---

*Race: AP = Asian-Pacific; H = Hispanic; W = White

Appendix II

Women's Political Organizations

CENTER FOR THE AMERICAN WOMAN AND POLITICS
Eagleton Institute of Politics
Rutgers University, New Brunswick, NJ 08901
(201) 932-9384

LEAGUE OF WOMEN VOTERS OF THE UNITED STATES
1730 M Street, NW
Washington, DC 20036
(202) 429-1965

NATIONAL ORGANIZATION FOR WOMEN
1401 New York Avenue, NW, Suite 800
Washington, DC 20005
(202) 347-2279

NATIONAL POLITICAL CONGRESS OF BLACK WOMEN
2025 I Street, NW, Suite 918
Washington, DC 20006
(202) 429-8716

NATIONAL WOMEN'S EDUCATION FUND
1410 Q Street, NW
Washington, DC 20009
(202) 462-8606

NATIONAL WOMEN'S POLITICAL CAUCUS
1275 K Street, NW, Suite 750
Washington, DC 20005
(202) 898-11000

WOMEN'S CAUCUS FOR POLITICAL SCIENCE
C/O American Political Science Association
1527 New Hampshire Avenue, NW
Washington, DC 20036
(202) 483-2512

WOMEN'S CAMPAIGN FUND
1724 I Street, NW, Suite 515
Washington, DC 20006
(202) 296-5346

(Information supplied by the Center for the American Woman and Politics.)

Bibliography

Baxter, Sandra, and Lansing, Margaret. *Women and Politics: The Visible Majority* (rev.ed.). Ann Arbor: University of Michigan Press, 1983.
Booth, Alice Lynn. *Careers in Politics for the New Woman*. New York: Franklin Watts, 1978.
Caroll, Susan J. *Women as Candidates in American Politics*. Bloomington: Indiana University Press, 1985.
Kirkpatrick, Jeane J. *Political Woman*. New York: Basic Books, 1974.
Lee, Rebecca K. *Republican Women Are Wonderful: A History of Women at Republican National Conventions*. Washington, DC: National Women's Political Caucus, 1980.
Mandel, Ruth B. *In the Running: The New Woman Candidate*. Boston: Beacon Press, 1983.
Martin, George. *Madame Secretary, Frances Perkins*. Boston: Houghton Mifflin, 1976.
Novick, Lee. *Democratic Women Are Wonderful: A History of Women at Democratic National Conventions*. Washington, DC: National Women's Political Caucus, 1980.
Romney, Ronna, and Harrison, Beppie. *Momentum: Women in American Politics Now*. New York: Crown Publishers, 1988.
Sheldon, Susanne E. and Roger. *Women in Government*. Lincolnwood, IL: VGM Horizons, 1983.
Smeal, Eleanor. *Why and How Women Will Elect the Next President*. New York: Harper & Row, 1984. (Contains an extensive bibliography.)
Tolchin, Susan and Martin. *Clout—Womenpower in Politics*. New York: Coward McCann, 1974.
Trafton, Barbara M. *Women Winning: How to Run for Office*. Boston: Harvard Common Press, 1984.

Index

A
aides
  congressional, 11, 17
  legislative, 29, 31, 82, 103
Alverno College, 27-28
American Association of
  University Women, 48
American Legion, 33
American Political Science
  Association (APSA), 35
Americans for Democratic Action, 9
APSA Congressional Fellowship, 35

B
Backer, Gracia, 63
Bailey, Patricia Price, 30, 63
Bailor, David, 18
Bell, Suzanne, 15
Bird, Rose, 64-66
blacks
  in American leadership, 28
  in office, 5, 56
  in politics, 64
Bojar, Karen, 53
Boosalis, Helen, 73, 75
Brasile, Donna, 64
Brough, Jean Marie, 63
Brown, Jerry, 64-65, 66

C
campaign
  manager, 2, 7, 64
  Presidential, 31
  strategy, 45-46
  timing of, 41, 42
Campbell, Jane, 9
Carlow College, 27-28
Center for the American Woman
  and Politics, 28, 34, 46, 61
Chavez, Linda, 84
Chisholm, Shirley, 5, 63, 89-91
city controller, 48, 70
city council, 41, 58, 74, 83, 104
civil service, 99, 102
Close Up Foundation, 17-18
college, 2, 23-32, 99
Collins, Cardiss, 5
Collins, Martha Layne, 73
committee member, 40, 51, 53, 54-55, 67, 69
committees, congressional, 16, 19, 35, 91, 93
conflict, in politics, 9, 25, 26, 42, 49, 68
Congressional Seminar, 18-20
  Advanced, 29
Constitution, U.S., 23-24
Corrigan, Mark, 16
county commissioner, 56, 104

INDEX

Crabb, Juanita, 58
Curry, Kathleen, 48

D
Delco, Wilhelmina, 53–54
Democratic Party, 3, 15, 31, 73, 83
Denker, Amy, 16, 17, 18
district attorney, 56, 94
Dole, Elizabeth Hanford, 4, 101
Douglass College, 27–28
Dukakis, Michael, 2, 104

E
Eagleton Fellowships, 34
Eagleton Institute of Politics, 28, 34, 105
EMILY (Early Money Is Like Yeast), 9

F
Falkenberry, Chris, 19
family vs. elective office, 1, 3, 8, 26, 37, 70, 106
Federal Forum, 29
Federal Trade Commission, 4, 30, 63
Feinstein, Dianne, 58–60
fellowships, 34–35
Ferguson, Miriam, 73
Ferraro, Geraldine, 95–97, 106
Financial Aid for Higher Education, 33
Ford, Gerald R., 4, 34
fund-raising, 8, 9, 41, 42, 47–48, 54, 64, 68, 70, 75, 76, 79, 92, 96, 100

G
Gabel, Mary Ann, 52, 54–56
Goucher College, 27–28
governorship, 1, 2, 9, 59, 73–77
Grace, Jean, 57–58

Grasso, Ella, 73

H
Hagarty, Lois, 31, 99
Harper, Ruth B., 62, 66–69
Hawkins, Paula, 47
high school, 2, 12–13, 99
 junior, 2, 11–12
Holmberg, Joyce, 63
House of Representatives, U.S., 1, 5, 8, 14, 19, 35, 76, 81, 83, 85–87, 91, 95, 102, 103

I
incumbency, vs. open seat, 41, 64
internship
 government, 24, 35, 103
 public leadership, 29
issues, 75, 91
 activist, 42
 domestic, 80, 85, 94
 "gut," 51, 85
 knowing, 46
 legal, 24
 women's, 2, 46, 53, 70, 84, 87, 100

J
Johnson, Lyndon Baines, 4
Jordan, Barbara, 5, 57

K
Kassebaum, Nancy L., 61, 80, 81–83
Katz, Vera, 63–64
Keesler, Oreon, 33
Kennedy, John F., 13
Kessler, Gladys, 30
Kirland, Howard, 20
Kirkpatrick, Jeane, 9, 38, 39, 40–41, 45, 46, 49, 95–96, 106
Kunin, Madeleine, 9, 73, 74, 75–77

INDEX 125

L
Lake, Celinda, 5, 64
Landon, Alfred M., 81
Landrieu, Mary, 64
law degree, 5, 30-31, 38, 91
leadership qualities, 11, 13, 28, 29, 35, 38, 40, 64
League of Women Voters, 102
Lewis, Ann, 9
lieutenant governorship, 76, 86
Lincoln, Evelyn, 13
Lindelow, Mimi, 31
lobbying, 16, 23, 29, 100, 101-102
Lockwood, Belva Ann, 1

M
Malcolm, Ellen, 9
Mandel, Ruth, 46
Manzer, Dr. Edna, 21-22
Martin, Lynn, 85
Marymount Manhattan College, 27-28
Mautner, Martha, 30
mayoralty, 2, 4, 8, 56-60, 104
Mayors, U.S. Conference of, 75
McConnell, Mitch, 20
media, 34, 103
  coverage by, 12, 24, 53
  getting message to, 46, 47, 48-49
  jobs in, 99, 104
Mikulski, Barbara, 8, 81, 83-85, 90
Miller, Melody, 13-14
Mofford, Rose, 73, 77
Momentum: Women in American Politics Now, 32, 59
Montgomery County Community College, 23-24
Morella, Constance A., 85-86
Mount Vernon College, 27-28
mud-slinging, 49, 84
Myrick, Sue, 8

myths, about women in politics, 37-38

N
Nagel, Dr. Jack, 25-27, 68
National League of Cities, 53
National Women's Education Fund, 29
National Women's Political Caucus, 48, 67, 84, 87, 100
Newsweek, 15
NOW (National Organization for Women), 37, 48, 100, 101
nursing, 30, 38

O
O'Connor, Sandra Day, 14, 30, 94-95, 103
old-boy network, 47, 73
O'Neill, Thomas ("Tip"), 51
open seat, 41, 74
Orr, Kay, 73-75
Otzel, Anne Marie, 14-15

P
page, legislative, 14-15
patronage, 25-26
Patterson, Liz, 85, 86
Pennsylvania, University of, 24
Perkins, Frances, 100-101
Perry, Carrie Saxon, 4, 7, 56-57
Pertschuk, Michael, 4
PLEN (Public Leadership Education Network), 27, 28, 29
political action committee, 47-48
political science, 2, 23, 69
  curriculum, 24-25, 26, 30
Political Woman, 9, 38
Presidency, U.S., 1, 4, 24, 89-91, 106
Presidential Classroom, 15-16, 29

publicity, 47, 53, 95
public office
  appointive, 28, 99–104
  elective, 28, 94, 96, 97
  local, 51–60, 85
  national, 79–87
  running for, 1–2, 37–43, 45–49
  state, 61–71, 79

R
Ray, Dixy Lee, 73
Republican Party, 3, 15, 31, 61, 70, 73, 83
role model, 5, 12, 15, 28
Roosevelt, Franklin D., 81, 100–101
Ross, Nellie Tayloe, 73
Rutgers, the State University, 27, 28, 34, 46, 105

S
Saiki, Patricia, 86–87
St. Catherine, College of, 27–28
scholarship, 20–21, 33
school board, 38, 51, 53, 56
Schroeder, Patricia, 91–94, 96, 106
Schuhl, Marc, 99
Secretary of Labor, 4, 100–101
Secretary of State, 77
Secretary of Transportation, 4, 101
seminar, political, 2, 11–12, 15–16, 17–20, 29, 34
Senate, U.S., 1, 8, 14, 19, 35, 39, 47, 61. 81, 102, 103
sex discrimination, 3, 5, 8, 26, 102–103
Siaughter, Louise M., 87
Smeal, Eleanor, 31, 37–39, 41, 45, 48–49
Smith, Dorothy, 55
Solein, Stephanie, 32
special-interest group, 28, 48, 99–100
Spelman College, 27–28
state legislator, 1, 2, 5, 8, 9, 14, 38, 40, 41, 49, 53, 56, 61, 66–71, 85, 86, 87, 91, 95, 99–104
state treasurer, 64
Stephens College, 27–28
Strause, Annette, 57
student government, 2, 7, 11, 13, 16–17
Supreme Court, U.S., 1, 23
  Justice, 24, 30, 94–95, 103
Supreme Court, state, 65–66

T
teaching, 21, 30, 38, 86, 89–90
Thatcher, Margaret, 97–98
toughness, mental, 3, 7, 8, 9, 40, 45, 76, 79, 105
trade-offs, 3, 13, 42
Trafton, Barbara, 40, 41, 45–46
Travis, Alice, 48

U
United States Youth Program, 33

V
Veterans of Foreign Wars, 20–21
Vice Presidency, 95, 106
Voice of Democracy contest, 20–21
volunteers, 2, 7, 15, 25, 37, 39, 40, 45, 82, 84, 94, 99–100, 102, 104
voter registration, 28, 54

W
Wallace, Lurleen, 73
Washington Workshops, 2, 11, 18–19, 20, 29
Wells College, 27–28
Weston, Frances, 66, 68, 69–70,

106
White House Fellowships, 34–35
Whitmere, Katherine, 57
Why and How Women Will Elect the Next President, 37–38
Women in Municipal government (WIMG), 53
Women in Public Policy Seminar, 29–30
Women's Campaign Fund, 5, 64, 84
Women Winning: How to Run for Office, 40

16054